Computer
Languages

TIME
LIFE ®
BOOKS

Other Publications:
AMERICAN COUNTRY
VOYAGE THROUGH THE UNIVERSE
THE THIRD REICH
THE TIME-LIFE GARDENER'S GUIDE
MYSTERIES OF THE UNKNOWN
TIME FRAME
FIX IT YOURSELF
FITNESS, HEALTH & NUTRITION
SUCCESSFUL PARENTING
HEALTHY HOME COOKING
LIBRARY OF NATIONS
THE ENCHANTED WORLD
THE KODAK LIBRARY OF CREATIVE PHOTOGRAPHY
GREAT MEALS IN MINUTES
THE CIVIL WAR
PLANET EARTH
COLLECTOR'S LIBRARY OF THE CIVIL WAR
THE EPIC OF FLIGHT
THE GOOD COOK
WORLD WAR II
HOME REPAIR AND IMPROVEMENT
THE OLD WEST

This volume is one of a series that examines
various aspects of computer technology
and the role computers play in modern life.

COVER
Like a network of superhighways, computer
languages link a programmer's human-style
commands to the electronic circuits that govern
the operations of a modern digital computer.

Computer Languages

BY THE EDITORS OF TIME-LIFE BOOKS

TIME-LIFE BOOKS, ALEXANDRIA, VIRGINIA

Contents

The Tortuous Path of Early Programming

In the perpetual darkness more than two miles below the surface of the North Atlantic, a submersible sled slowly traced the alpine contours of the ocean bottom in the summer of 1985. Named the *Argo* after the ship in which the legendary Greek hero Jason sought the Golden Fleece, the 16-foot-long craft resembled a section of scaffolding flung on its side and stuffed with equipment — powerful lights, sonar, video cameras. Far above, arrayed in front of a video screen in the control room of the U.S. Navy research vessel *Knorr*, members of a joint French-American scientific expedition intently watched the images transmitted by the submersible as it was towed above a desolate landscape of canyons and mud slides.

After 16 days of patient search, a scattering of metallic debris appeared on the screen, followed by the unmistakable outline of a ship's boiler. A jubilant cry rose from the scientists. The ocean liner *Titanic*, sunk 73 years earlier with more than 1,500 of its 2,200 passengers still on board, had finally been found.

The quest for the remains of the *Titanic* in the crushing depths of the sea was a remarkable application of computer technology, as exotic in its means as in its venue. Not least of the keys to the successful outcome was the agility of modern computer programming.

Argo's ensemble of sonar, lights and cameras was orchestrated by an array of computers that were each programmed in a different computer language. The computer on the unmanned *Argo* itself was programmed in FORTH, a concise but versatile language originally designed to regulate the movement of telescopes and also used to control devices and processes ranging from heart monitors to special-effects video cameras. The computer on the *Knorr* was programmed in C, a powerful but rather cryptic language (its appearance has been likened to that of the typographical profanities uttered by comic-strip characters) capable of precisely specifying computer operations. The telemetry system at either end of the finger-thick coaxial cable connecting the two vessels, which in effect enabled their computers to "talk" to each other, was programmed in a third, rudimentary tongue known as assembly language.

Programming languages are the carefully and ingeniously conceived sequences of words, letters, numerals and abbreviated mnemonics used by people to communicate with their computers. Without them, computers and their allied equipment would be just so much useless hardware. Each language is regulated by its own grammar and syntax. A programming language that approximates human language and can generate more than one instruction with a single statement is deemed to be "high-level." But computer languages tend to be much more sober and precise than human languages. They do not indulge in multiple

The earliest computer languages forced programmers to follow a tortuous semantic path in order to issue even simple commands. The phrase in this illustration, written in the cryptic notation called assembly language, instructs a computer to store (ST) the number 5 in memory under the label BSUM.

meanings, inflections or twists of irony. Like computers themselves, computer languages have no sense of humor.

Today there are several hundred such languages, considerably more than a thousand if their variations, called dialects, are counted. They enable their users to achieve a multitude of purposes, from solving complex mathematical problems and manipulating (or "crunching") business statistics to creating musical scores and computer graphics. No existing language is perfect for every situation. The choice among them usually is determined by one or more of three factors: The language is convenient for the programmer; it is usable on the available computer; it is well suited to the problem at hand. The multiple tongues employed on the *Titanic* expedition are a case in point. For the computers aboard the surface ship *Knorr,* C was the preferred language because it provided more direct control of the computerized hardware. FORTH was the only high-level language that could be used on the submersible *Argo's* computer. And the precise timing required of the signals passed by cable between the two vessels was best accomplished by rigid assembly language.

As varied as languages have become, they all build on a common base. At their most fundamental level, computers respond to only a single language— the high and low electric voltages representing the ones and zeros of binary code. Depending on how these signals are fed into the computer, they can mean many different things. A particular combination of ones and zeros might indicate a location in the computer's memory. Another might be a piece of data to be processed.

Yet another collection of binary digits, or bits, might command the machine to perform a certain action, such as adding two numbers. The circuitry of each type of computer is designed to respond to a specific and finite set of these binary-encoded commands, which may be combined and recombined to enable the machine to perform a vast range of tasks. Though straightforward enough, this so-called machine code is a forbidding, alien language to human beings. A computer program of any size, in its machine-code form, consists of thousands or even millions of ones and zeros, strung together like beads on a seemingly interminable string. A mistake in even one of these digits can make the difference between a program's success and failure.

Less than half a century ago, machine code was the only means of communicating with computers. Since then, generations of language designers have harnessed the power of the computer to make it serve as its own translator. Now, when a programmer uses the command PRINT "HELLO" or the statement LET A = B * (C - D) in a program, a translating program is called into action, converting those commands into the ones and zeros that a machine can understand.

PAPER TAPE AND PLUG-BOARDS
The methods used to program the world's first general-purpose computers were as cumbersome and primitive as the machines they served. The historic Mark I, assembled at Harvard University during World War II, was a five-ton conglomeration of relays, shafts, gears and dials, 51 feet long. It received its instructions for solving problems from spools of punched paper tape that were prepared and fed into the computer by a small corps of technicians. A more advanced ma-

chine, ENIAC (for Electronic Numerical Integrator and Computer), was completed in 1945 at the University of Pennsylvania's Moore School of Electrical Engineering. Unlike the Harvard Mark I, which was electromechanical, ENIAC was fully electronic. But it was still devilishly difficult to program. Its primary developers, physicist John W. Mauchly and engineer J. Presper Eckert, had responded to the urgencies of wartime by concentrating on ENIAC's hardware. Programming took a back seat. ENIAC was not even equipped to receive instructions on paper tape. To prepare it for operation, a team of technicians had to set thousands of switches by hand and insert hundreds of cables into plugboards until the front of the computer resembled a mass of spaghetti. Not surprisingly, ENIAC's users tried to squeeze the last drop of information out of any given programming configuration before they undertook to change it.

These early experiences made it all too plain that a better means of communicating with the machine was needed if computers were to approach their potential. And even as ENIAC hummed through its first electronic calculations, some forward-looking work on a higher level of programming was being done elsewhere. In at least one case, however, many years would pass before the results came to light.

THE PLAN CALCULUS
Konrad Zuse's world was crashing down around him early in 1945 as the Allied military noose tightened on Berlin, his home city. The young German engineer had been working since before the war on a series of relatively small, general-purpose computers, using the living room of his parents' apartment as his laboratory. Zuse's efforts were a notable example of parallel yet independent developments in science; he had no idea of the similar progress being made in other nations, and his own government had shown little interest in his computer work. Shortly before the fall of Berlin, Zuse loaded his only surviving computer, dubbed the Z4, onto a wagon and fled with a convoy of other refugees to a small town in the Bavarian Alps.

During the grim years immediately after the war, Zuse found himself without either funds or facilities to work on computer hardware. Turning his energies to theory instead, he sought a better way to program a computer — not specifically the Z4, but any similar machine. What was needed, he decided, was a system of symbolic and numeric notations based on logical sequence — in effect a calculus of problem-solving steps.

Working alone, Zuse devised a programming system that he named Plan Calculus, or, in German, Plankalkül. He wrote a manuscript explaining his creation and applying it to a variety of problems, including sorting numbers and doing arithmetic by means of binary notation (other computers of the day operated in decimal). He also taught himself to play chess and then produced 49 pages of program fragments in Plankalkül that would allow a computer to assess a player's position. "It was interesting for me to test the efficiency and general scope of the Plankalkül," Zuse later wrote, "by applying it to chess problems."

Zuse never expected to see his language actually run on a computer. "The Plankalkül," he wrote, "arose purely as a piece of desk work, without regard to whether or not machines suitable for Plankalkül programs would be available in

In 1985, programmers employed a trio of languages — C, FORTH and assembly language — to give the world its first glimpse of the wrecked *Titanic* since the ill-fated ocean liner sank beneath the Atlantic 73 years earlier. Guided by image-enhancing and camera-control programs written in the three languages, a submersible camera sled passed digitized pictures to the research ship *Knorr* up 13,000 feet of pressure-protected cable from the *Titanic's* quiet grave *(left)*.

the foreseeable future." Although he briefly visited the United States in the late 1940s, only small portions of his manuscript were published, much less implemented, in the decade after the war; many of his ideas for a systematic, logical language remained unknown to an entire generation of computer linguists. Not until 1972 did Zuse's full manuscript appear in print. Its publication prompted experts to wonder what effect Plankalkül would have had if it had been disseminated earlier. "It shows us how different things might have been," one critic of subsequent languages has noted, " — how what we have today is not necessarily the best of all possible worlds."

While Zuse was laboring in isolation, a collegial effort to develop a programming language for real machines was under way at academic centers in Great Britain and the United States, where the earliest computers were beginning to be used. But progress was slow. Not only did each computer have its own machine code and programming method, but developing the machines themselves required the lion's share of the scientists' time and talent.

During the years immediately after the war, most programmers continued to work in machine code—the binary digits that correspond to a computer's circuits. To make the job slightly easier, some of them began using shorthand number systems to denote combinations of bits (pages 12-13), a method akin to a stenographer's using symbols to represent words when taking dictation. The first of these systems was base eight, also known as octal. Just as there are only two digits, 0 and 1, in the binary system, there are eight in octal—the numerals 0 through 7. Each of these octal numbers is used to represent one of eight possible combinations of three bits (000, 001, 010, 011, 100, 101, 110 and 111). A more ambitious numbering system that followed, base 16, or hexadecimal (hex, to programmers), gathered bits into groups of four. The 16 possible combinations of four bits were represented by the numerals 0 through 9 and the letters A through F.

Writing in Plankalkül, the language he designed as a young refugee in the Bavarian Alps just after World War II, Konrad Zuse scribbled a chess-playing program on sheets of graph paper — here, a list of steps to determine whether the white king is in jeopardy. Now recognized as the first high-level computer language, the innovative Plankalkül remained obscure for decades while Zuse devoted his attention to building a computer-manufacturing business.

A PENCHANT FOR GADGETS

To at least one frustrated American programmer, the modest progress offered by such number systems seemed grossly insufficient. Grace Murray Hopper was accustomed to being in the vanguard. She had grown up fascinated by things mechanical — "gadgets," she called them. As a girl of seven, she had taken apart all the wind-up alarm clocks in her family's summer home in New Hampshire — to discover how they worked — and could not put them back together. The disciplining that followed failed to dim her scientific enthusiasm. After graduating with honors from Vassar College in 1928, she earned a Ph.D. in mathematics at Yale — a rare achievement then for a woman — and returned to Vassar to teach.

At the height of World War II, Hopper joined the U.S. Naval Reserve, and in June 1944 she earned her commission. Standing just over five feet tall and weighing 105 pounds, she was surely the smallest officer in the navy.

But her contribution through the years would be prodigious. Lieutenant (jg) Hopper was assigned to the navy team that was developing programs for the Mark I at Harvard. "Mark I was the biggest, prettiest gadget I'd ever seen," she said later.

The programming team Hopper joined consisted of two male ensigns; she subsequently learned that when the men heard that a "gray-haired old college professor" was coming, one of them bribed the other so that he would not have to take the desk next to hers. Hopper soon proved her worth as a programmer, however. "I had an edge," she said. "I had studied engineering as well as mathematics, and I knew how the machine worked from the beginning. Of course, I was lucky. When I graduated in 1928, I didn't know there was going to be a computer in 1944."

In 1949, a civilian again, Hopper joined the fledgling Eckert-Mauchly Computer Corporation, which was operating out of an old factory in North Philadelphia. Mauchly and Eckert had left the University of Pennsylvania's Moore School in 1946 after a bitter fight over patent rights to their electronic computers. Once in business for themselves, they secured several contracts and set about building a new machine that they hoped would prove the commercial viability of computing. They called their machine the Universal Automatic Computer, or UNIVAC.

THE HIDDEN PERILS OF OCTAL
Grace Hopper had dutifully learned how to work in octal, teaching herself to add, subtract, multiply and even divide in the strange system. "The entire establishment was firmly convinced that the only way to write an efficient program was in octal," she later lamented (the prevailing view was that the computer's time was more valuable than the programmer's; if a program could be executed swiftly, the difficulty of writing it was immaterial). And indeed octal proved very helpful in getting the company's prototype computer up and running. But Hopper found that it was causing confusion in another area of her life. She was having trouble balancing her personal bank account — an embarrassing dilemma for a trained mathematician. Finally, she appealed to her brother, who was a banker, and after several evenings' work he solved the mystery: Occasionally she was subtracting a check in octal rather than in the decimal system that the bank — and everyone else — used. "I faced the problem of living in two different worlds," Hopper said. "That may have been one of the things that motivated me to get rid of octal as much as possible."

Hopper's efforts to ease the programmer's burden (and keep her checkbook balanced) would eventually shape the course of computing. But she was not alone in the attempt. Shortly before she came to Philadelphia, John Mauchly made a suggestion that would take programming a first tentative step beyond both octal and hexadecimal. He directed his programmers to devise a computer language that would allow a person to enter problems into the machine in algebraic terms — an approach that Konrad Zuse would have approved of. By the end of 1949, the system, known as Short Code, was operational. Later promoted as an "electronic dictionary," it was a primitive high-level language — and a definite improvement over machine code. A programmer first wrote the problem to be solved in the form of mathematical equations and then used a printed table

The Language of Numbers

At bottom, computers understand only one language — the binary code of ones and zeros that represent on-off electronic pulses. Because this code is so unwieldy for humans, programmers have devised more concise ways of expressing the binary numbers that constitute, for example, the contents of a computer's memory or the address in memory of each piece of data. Two numbering systems that can serve as convenient shorthand for the binary (base 2) system are octal (base 8) and hexadecimal (base 16). Because 8 is 2 raised to the third power ($8 = 2 \times 2 \times 2$), one octal digit is the equivalent of three binary digits; similarly, one hexadecimal digit represents four binary digits (16 is 2 raised to the fourth power). The tables below list the decimal numbers 0 through 16 and their binary, octal and hexadecimal equivalents. In each system, the value of a digit is determined by the value of its place column. The letters A through F in hexadecimal represent the 11th through 16th digits in that system.

Four Systems with Different Bases

DECIMAL

PLACE 100	PLACE 10	PLACE 1
		0
		1
		2
		3
		4
		5
		6
		7
		8
		9
	1	0
	1	1
	1	2
	1	3
	1	4
	1	5
	1	6

BINARY

PLACE 32	PLACE 16	PLACE 8	PLACE 4	PLACE 2	PLACE 1
					0
					1
				1	0
				1	1
			1	0	0
			1	0	1
			1	1	0
			1	1	1
		1	0	0	0
		1	0	0	1
		1	0	1	0
		1	0	1	1
		1	1	0	0
		1	1	0	1
		1	1	1	0
		1	1	1	1
	1	0	0	0	0

OCTAL

PLACE 64	PLACE 8	PLACE 1
		0
		1
		2
		3
		4
		5
		6
		7
	1	0
	1	1
	1	2
	1	3
	1	4
	1	5
	1	6
	1	7
	2	0

HEXADECIMAL

PLACE 256	PLACE 16	PLACE 1
		0
		1
		2
		3
		4
		5
		6
		7
		8
		9
		A
		B
		C
		D
		E
		F
	1	0

The Process of Conversion

DECIMAL TO BINARY

Subtract the highest possible power of 2 from the decimal number — here, 4 from 5 — and continue subtracting the highest possible power from the remainder, marking a 1 in each binary place column where subtraction occurs and a 0 where it does not. Here, one 4, no 2 and one 1 gives binary 101.

BINARY TO DECIMAL

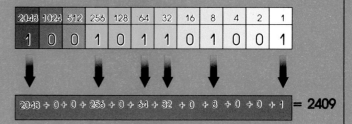

Add the values of all the binary places occupied by 1s. Here, to convert the 12-digit binary number 100101101001, add the place values 2048, 256, 64, 32, 8 and 1. The result is the decimal number 2409.

BINARY TO OCTAL

Starting with the rightmost digit, group the binary digits in threes, treating each trio as a separate binary number with the place values 4, 2 and 1. The sum of each trio's place values equals one octal digit. Here, the sums of the values of each of the four groups are 4, 5, 5 and 1, making octal 4551.

BINARY TO HEXADECIMAL

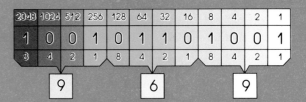

Again from the right, group the binary digits in fours, treating each quartet as a separate binary number with the place values 8, 4, 2 and 1. The sum of each group's place values equals one hexadecimal digit. Here, the sums of the values of each of the three groups are 9, 6 and 9, making hexadecimal 969.

The Principles of Addition

4	2	1
	¹0	1
	1	1
1	0	0

+

8	1
¹6	7
0	1
7	0

+

16	1
¹D	7
O	9
E	0

+

Addition in binary. Using the same rules as in decimal addition, start by adding the figures in the rightmost, or 1s, column: 1 + 1. The result — 2 — is expressed in binary as 10 (one-zero). Write down the 0 and carry the 1. In the 2s column, 1 + 1 again equals 2, or binary 10; write down the 0 and carry the 1 into the 4s column. The result is 100, the binary equivalent of decimal 4.

Addition in octal. Adding the figures in the 1s column — 7 + 1 — gives 8, expressed in the octal system as 10 (one-zero). As in binary addition, write down the 0 and carry the 1. Next, add the figures in the 8s column; the sum of 6 and 1 is 7. The result is octal 70 — the equivalent of binary 111000, or decimal 56.

Addition in hexadecimal. Adding the figures in the 1s column — 7 + 9 — gives 16, the base of the hexadecimal system, expressed as 10. Write down the 0 and carry the 1. In the 16s column, add the 1 to D (13 in decimal). D plus 1 is E (14 in decimal). The result is E0 (E-zero), hexadecimal shorthand for binary 11100000, or decimal 224.

to translate these equations symbol by symbol into two-character codes. For instance, a parenthesis became 09, while the plus symbol became 07. A separate program in the computer then converted these codes to zeros and ones, and the machine performed the appropriate functions.

Short Code's partner program was essentially a primitive "interpreter," a language translator that converts the high-level statements in which a program is written into simpler instructions for immediate execution. As programming languages evolved, interpreters would become one of the two basic categories of language translators.

Short Code was soon overtaken by new advances in languages, but its central idea endured. Far from being simply glorified adding machines, computers are consummate manipulators of symbols, whether those symbols represent numbers, letters, colors or even musical notes. A computer has no difficulty taking the code numerals 07 and performing the sequence of steps that leads it to add two numbers, as long as it has been programmed to recognize 07 as the symbol for addition. In the same manner, it can take a complete statement, such as IF N < 100 THEN PRINT N/47, and translate it into the basic machine instructions that will enable the hardware to carry out the desired task. This purposeful manipulation of symbols is the fundamental principle behind all programming languages.

Although Short Code was never a commercial success, the language made a deep impression on Grace Hopper. "Short Code was the first step toward something which gave a programmer the power to write a program in a language that bore no resemblance whatsoever to the original machine code," she said. But before the promise of Short Code could be realized, much more had to be done.

THE BRITISH CONTRIBUTION

The pace of progress in computer languages was tightly bound to advances in computer hardware, and during the late 1940s there were few such advances. Most of them were influenced by Mauchly and Eckert's early work and could in fact trace their origins to a specific event: a series of lectures held at the Moore School in the summer of 1946. There Mauchly and Eckert discussed the successor to ENIAC they were then planning. Dubbed the Electronic Discrete Variable Automatic Computer, or EDVAC, it would dramatically reduce the labor involved in changing from one program to another by storing its programs and data electronically in an expanded internal memory.

One participant that summer was Maurice V. Wilkes, then head of the Mathematical Laboratory at Cambridge University. Inspired by the lectures, Wilkes returned to England and set about designing a machine based on the EDVAC concept; construction began in 1947. Named the Electronic Delay Storage Automatic Calculator, or EDSAC, it became operational in 1949—well before Mauchly and Eckert's firm produced its first commercial computer.

Like many early computers, EDSAC was a finicky performer. One programmer recalled that even the sound of an airplane flying overhead could bring it to a halt. Whenever EDSAC was shut down for any reason, a set of "initial orders" had to be loaded into the machine to enable it to accept programs again. This process made a whirring sound, which was a signal for everyone who wanted to use the computer to come running, programs in hand. Those fortunate enough to have offices nearest the computer usually ended up in the front of the queue. The others might have a long wait.

At first, EDSAC could perform 18 basic operations (modern computers usually have a repertoire of more than 200), each of them triggered by a particular sequence of ones and zeros. Early on, EDSAC's designers decided not to force its programmers to use only this machine code in their programs. Instead they set up a system of mnemonics in which each machine instruction was represented by a single capital letter. Thus *S* meant "Subtract," *I* meant "Read the next row of holes on the input paper tape," *T* meant "Transfer information to storage" and *Z* meant "Stop the machine." When a programmer typed a mnemonic on a specially adapted keyboard, the corresponding binary instruction was punched into a paper tape, which could then be fed to the machine.

BUILDING A LIBRARY

Even more valuable than the mnemonics devised for EDSAC was the library of subroutines set up for the machine. Subroutines were already a familiar concept in computing: Grace Hopper and her colleagues had used them on the Harvard Mark I during the war. But they continued to pose their own peculiar problems. Subroutines are independent sections of a computer program that are used over and over and are called for by the main program when needed. For instance, one subroutine might calculate the square root of a number; another might enable a computer to display a character on a monitor. Early programmers often kept notebooks containing commonly used subroutines so that they did not have to start from scratch when one was needed. The problem was that the addresses that designated where each of a subroutine's instructions and variables were to reside in memory changed according to where the subroutine occurred in a program.

The tailoring of subroutines for different positions within a program was an obvious candidate for automation, and this was first accomplished on EDSAC. The programmers at Cambridge began by writing a collection of generalized subroutines that together formed a subroutine library. After that, a programmer had only to enter a short command, and the computer would do the work of adapting the subroutine to its particular place in the program.

Maurice Wilkes called the EDSAC scheme of mnemonics and subroutines an assembly system, since it assembled sequences of subroutines, and the name stuck. Today, any programming language in which each short mnemonic directly represents one machine instruction is known as an assembly language. A program called an assembly program, or an assembler for short, converts the mnemonics of the assembly language directly into the binary sequences of machine code *(pages 23-35)*.

Assembly language remains in use today because of its close relationship to the machine; indeed, an assembly language is machine-specific, designed to correspond to the set of machine-code instructions wired into a particular computer's central processing unit. Thus, assembly language is a favorite of programmers who want to compress their programs into the smallest possible space in memory and have them run as fast and efficiently as possible. These attributes made it ideal for programming the telemetry system used in the *Titanic* search to send signals between the surface vessel's control room and the underwater sled. But assembly language also has some disadvantages. Being closer to the machine's language than to natural language, it is a difficult medium in which to work. Anyone writing in assembly language has to be intimately familiar with how a computer does things — to know, for example, the many steps required simply to add two numbers. Moreover, because assembly language is machine-specific, a program written in one machine's assembly language is gibberish to a computer of a different type.

For these reasons, an ill-conceived assembly language can be more trouble than it is worth, yet just such a flawed attempt at assembly language led to one of the next major developments in programming. The language was the brainchild of a superb mathematician, Alan M. Turing. Turing was the prolific young genius of Great Britain's first ventures into computer science. In 1936, at the age of 25, he had described — in the abstract — a "universal machine" that could solve almost any logical or mathematical problem presented to it.

By 1948, Turing was in charge of programming the prototype of a real computer. Called the Mark I, the machine was being constructed at the University of Manchester, in the north of England (and was not related to the Mark I at Harvard). The Manchester Mark I used combinations of five binary digits to represent the machine's repertoire of instructions, with each instruction requiring four such combinations, or 20 bits. Intending to make the Mark I easier to program, Turing installed a system in which a mnemonic symbol was substituted for each of the 32 combinations of zeros and ones possible with a five-bit code. The symbols Turing assigned to the combinations were the letters, numerals and punctuation marks of a standard teleprinter keyboard. For example, a slash (/) — or "stroke" to the British — stood for 00000, or zero; an R stood for 01010, and so on up to a £, representing 11111.

SYMBOLIC DOGGEREL
The full set of symbols was: /E@A:SIU½DRJNFCKTZLWHYPQOBG"MXV£. Because the mnemonics followed no particular order, no one at Manchester, except possibly Turing himself, could memorize them. So the staff quickly invented a nonsensical bit of verse, based on the keyboard symbols, to help them remember. It went:

> stroke Edith at Aberdeen colon She Is Under half
> Dispense Royal Justice Napoleon For Charlie Knows Tall Zebras Laugh
> We Hear Young People Question On Best Grounds
> quotations for a thousand fifteen pounds

The doggerel worked, and many of the programmers at Manchester remembered it for the rest of their lives.

Unfortunately, in practice Turing's system was about as unwieldy as the verse it inspired. In the production version of the Mark I, the portion of the 20-bit machine instruction that designated the function to be performed was extended from five bits to six; thus, instead of being represented by one symbol, the function had to be represented by a pair of symbols, one of which also specified another part of the instruction. As a result, written programs were exceedingly difficult to decipher. Wilkes at Cambridge would later call it "bizarre in the extreme."

Programming's Antecedents

Languages for writing computer programs originated only after World War II, but the essence of programming itself can be traced back to antiquity. The Babylonian who, 3,800 years ago, inscribed a banking calculation on the tablet at right was writing an algorithm, or step-by-step procedure for solving a particular kind of problem. The scribe explained the procedure by presenting a specific example; others could substitute the appropriate numbers for their own calculations. Centuries later, Greek scholars described formal number-manipulating principles, but they employed ordinary human language, with all its potential ambiguities. Unambiguous symbolic notation was introduced with the algebraic method devised in the Arab world, but even this required the reader to deduce some of the steps involved in solving a given problem. Still, the kinship between ancient methods and those of the 20th century is evident when the historic algorithms shown here and on the following pages are translated into BASIC (below) and fed into a computer: The machine arrives at the same solutions as those once calculated by hand so long ago.

```
10      ' Set the interest rate to 20 percent.
20      LET RATE = .2
30      '
40      ' After one year the total is the original kur of grain plus
50      ' one year's interest payment.
60      LET YEARS = 1
70      LET GRAIN = 1 + RATE
80      '
90      ' Continue calculating the amount of grain after each year
100     ' until the goal of two kurs is met or exceeded.
110     WHILE GRAIN < 2
120          LET PREVIOUS = GRAIN
130          LET GRAIN = GRAIN * (1 + RATE)
140          LET YEARS = YEARS + 1
150     WEND
160     '
170     ' The goal of two kurs of grain was reached during the year
180     ' before the current value of YEARS. Next, calculate the
190     ' amount of interest month-by-month within the last year.
200     LET MONTHGAIN = (GRAIN − PREVIOUS)/12
210     LET MONTHNUMBER = (2 − PREVIOUS) /MONTHGAIN
220     '
230     PRINT "The grain will be doubled to two kurs after";
             YEARS − 1; "years and"; MONTHNUMBER; "months."
```

An ancient calculation. In cuneiform script, a Babylonian clay tablet dating from 1800 B.C. offers a procedure for figuring compound interest. The algorithm is expressed as a specific example, determining how many years and months it takes to double a certain quantity of grain called a *kur* at an annual interest rate of 20 percent (the grain served as currency). The BASIC program at left presents the same procedure in terms a computer can understand.

A Greek algorithm. This page from a 10th-century manuscript of Euclid's classic treatise *Elements* — a 13-volume work written by the Greek mathematician in the 3rd century B.C. — describes a method for finding the greatest common divisor of two numbers without using specific numbers in the explanation. The algorithm, also shown in the BASIC program below, is the earliest still in common use by computer scientists.

```
10    PRINT "Enter a counting number.": INPUT FSTNMBR
20    PRINT "Enter another counting number.": INPUT SECNDNMBR
30    '
40    ' Establish which is the larger number and which is the
50    ' smaller. (This also works if the two numbers are equal.)
60    IF FSTNMBR > = SECNDNMBR THEN BIG = FSTNMBR:
      SMALL = SECNDNMBR: ELSE BIG = SECNDNMBR:
      SMALL = FSTNMBR
70    '
80    ' Subtract the smaller number from the bigger number until
90    ' there is a remainder that is less than the smaller of the
100   ' two numbers. Let the remainder and the smaller number
110   ' replace the original two numbers from this point on.
120   WHILE (BIG MOD SMALL) <> 0
130        LET LEFTOVER = BIG MOD SMALL
140        LET BIG = SMALL
150        LET SMALL = LEFTOVER
160   WEND
170   '
180   PRINT "The largest number that divides"; FSTNMBR; "and";
      SECNDNMBR; "is"; SMALL; "."
```

Algebraic notation. A passage from Arabic mathematician al-Khwarizmi's textbook *Al-Jabr Wa-Al-Muqabala (The Science of Cancellation and Reduction)* solves the equation $x^2 + 10x = 39$ to illustrate a technique known as "completing the square." Written in Baghdad in 820 A.D., the book did much to shape the mathematics of the medieval world and led to the words "algebra" (from "Al-Jabr" in the title) and "algorithm" (from "al-Khwarizmi"). Below, a program written in BASIC demonstrates the steps al-Khwarizmi used to solve the equation.

```
10    PRINT "Enter the numerical part of the x-term:": INPUT XNUMBER
20    PRINT "Enter the right side of the equation:": INPUT RIGHTSIDE
30    '
40    ' First divide the numerical part of the x-term by 2.
50    ' In this case the numerical part is 10 and half of that is 5.
60    LET HALFXNUMBER = XNUMBER/2
70    '
80    ' The new number, 5, is squared and added to both sides of
90    ' the equation. The left side becomes x squared + 10x + 25,
100   ' which equals (x + 5) squared, and the right side becomes
110   ' 39 + 25, which is 64 or 8 squared.
120   LET NEWRIGHTSIDE = RIGHTSIDE + HALFXNUMBER *
      HALFXNUMBER
130   '
140   ' Next, take the positive square root of both sides,
150   ' which yields x + 5 = 8. Finally, solve for x by subtracting 5
160   ' from both sides.
170   IF NEWRIGHTSIDE < 0
      THEN PRINT "There are no real number values for x. ":END
180   LET X = SQR(NEWRIGHTSIDE) − HALFXNUMBER
190   '
200   PRINT "The number"; X; "solves the equation."
```

Manchester programmers were learning the hard way an adage that has become well established in computing: Design decisions made in the early stages of a project are very difficult to change later. Once the teleprinter notation was accepted, it influenced the choice of hardware to implement it and became entrenched in the system. It was even perpetuated on commercial versions of the Mark I later manufactured by a Manchester company.

But Turing's teleprinter notation did have one positive effect: It led to the creation of several high-level programming languages designed to make the Mark I easier to use. The first of these was the work of Alick E. Glennie, a young scientist who came to Manchester after completing a classified project in atomic-weapons research on EDSAC at Cambridge. In the summer of 1952, working in his spare time, Glennie devised a programming system called AUTOCODE that included one of the first high-level languages. Like Short Code, AUTOCODE allowed programmers to use mathematical symbols in their programs. Once these programs were entered into the Mark I, AUTOCODE translated them into a machine-code program that, when run, would perform the desired mathematical operations. But unlike a program written in Short Code, which needed its interpreter to translate it into machine code each time it was run, the machine-code program produced by Glennie's AUTOCODE system could be stored and run at any time.

In creating AUTOCODE, Glennie had become one of computing's first language designers. When asked later how best to approach the job, he answered wryly that the language designer should "put himself in the position of a teacher teaching a very backward child how to read." Largely because of Glennie's sensitive role in nuclear research, however, his work was never published, and in the end he was the only one ever to use AUTOCODE. It was a "successful but premature experiment," he later concluded. "The climate of thought was not right."

Indeed, most programmers of the time were decidedly unenthusiastic about systems like AUTOCODE. One reason for their negative attitude was the limitations of the available hardware. Programmers felt that they had to use machine code in order to coax as much speed as possible out of their recalcitrant machines. But there was another, more subtle reason. Early programmers were well aware — and proud — of their status as practitioners of a somewhat mysterious craft. As one of them put it, programmers were a kind of "priesthood," controlling access to the new and highly publicized machines. Systems like AUTOCODE, by making programming at least somewhat easier to do, threatened to open the temple doors to everyone.

PROGRAMS THAT WRITE PROGRAMS

The defenders of the priesthood were fighting a losing battle. At the beginning of the 1950s, the computer industry in both the United States and Great Britain was on the verge of tremendous growth: Entrepreneurs could clearly see a multitude of commercial and governmental, as well as scientific, uses for the fascinating new machines. Remington Rand (later Sperry Rand), an American firm that ranked second only to the International Business Machines Corporation in sales of mechanical office equipment, had acquired Mauchly and Eckert's company, providing a timely infusion of capital and marketing expertise. Mauch-

Navy Lieutenant Grace Hopper, working long hours in 1947 as one of the three programmers on the Harvard Mark I, glances up from a disorderly pile of engineering blueprints. Hopper, who went on to become one of the leading proponents of high-level computer languages, programmed the electromechanical Mark I in a rudimentary machine code.

ly and Eckert stayed in their jobs, as did their star programmer, Grace Hopper. And in 1951, Remington Rand delivered its first commercial computer, UNIVAC, to the U.S. Bureau of the Census.

That same year, Hopper was assigned to set up a library of standardized mathematical subroutines for UNIVAC. Wilkes and two other Cambridge programmers had just published a book on EDSAC's programming system (it was the first programming textbook ever written), and their assembly language became the envy of progressive programmers around the world. But Hopper resolved to go further. Drawing on her experience with Short Code, she and a team of programmers set about designing a system that would translate a program written in a high-level language into a machine-language program.

COMPLETING THE FOUNDATION

The translating program would handle in milliseconds a large part of the labor associated with programming: organizing subroutines, allocating computer memory, converting high-level commands. Hopper named this translating program a compiler. "The subroutines were in a library," she later explained, "and when you pull stuff out of a library you compile things. It's as simple as that."

Although Glennie's AUTOCODE at Manchester had similar features, Hopper's compiler was the first translating system to become widely known. In contrast to the line-by-line interpreter used by Short Code, Hopper's compiler converted the entire high-level program into machine code as a separate step. The coded program could then be run immediately or filed away for future use, as the programmer saw fit. The compiling program could even be removed from the computer before the compiled program was run, unlike an interpreting program, which had to run hand in hand with the program it was interpreting.

Now the two basic categories of high-level language, compiled and interpreted, were in place. The distinction between them remains an important one today, and it has not changed much since the words were coined. Modern compilers offer features that Hopper and her contemporaries could only dream of. But they still serve the basic function of translating an entire program written in a high-level language into a machine-code program that the computer can understand.

Hopper named her first compiler A-0, implying that it was as close to the beginning as one could get. As it was improved and expanded over the years, A-0 became A-1, then A-2 and A-3. When a version of the compiler was released to the public a few years later, the sales department at Remington Rand decided that it needed a catchier title, and it was renamed MATH-MATIC.

Work on translating systems, both compilers and interpreters, was under way elsewhere in the early 1950s. When IBM came out with its first fully electronic computer, the 701, in 1953, it offered an interpreted programming language called Speedcoding. About the same time, two young mathematicians named Niel Zierler and J. Halcombe Laning Jr. were writing a high-level programming language and translating system for the newly operative Whirlwind computer at the Massachusetts Institute of Technology. With their system, they achieved what John Mauchly had desired for Short Code: the ability to enter mathematical symbols directly into the computer in a fairly natural way. Whereas in Short Code an equation such as i = 10 was written as three pairs of two-digit codes (plus three pairs of leading zeros), in Laning and Zierler's system the equation was written simply as the statement i = 10.

PROGRAMMING IN ENGLISH

Grace Hopper, meanwhile, had set herself a new goal. She sensed, perhaps more fully than anyone else, that the spread of computers from laboratories to corporate accounting departments and government agencies would create an entirely new category of users. "We have a large variety of people out there who want to solve problems," she said. "Some of them are symbol-oriented, some of them are word-oriented, and they are going to need different kinds of languages rather than our trying to force them all into becoming mathematical logicians."

Acting on her vision, Hopper and her team set about devising a compiler that would allow people in business to program in a language that was as close as possible to everyday English. Instead of creating another language steeped in mathematical symbols, they sought one that permitted commands such as COMPARE and TRANSFER. After months of work, they settled on a list of about 30 such verbs that seemed to be the workhorses of data processing. Then they wrote a compiler that would translate programs written with these verbs into machine code. To make it easier for the compiler to recognize the verbs, Hopper's team adopted a technique that survived until recently in descendants of their language: Each of the verbs they selected had a unique combination of first and third letters — no two had the same combination — so the compiler could ignore all the other letters in the word while generating machine code.

By 1956, a prototype of the new compiler was ready. But before a single copy could be sold to customers, Hopper found that she would first have to sell management on the idea. Her bosses, as she later recalled, were reluctant to believe that a computer could understand words. Computers, after all, were dumb machines; teaching them English was as farfetched as trying to teach them to speak.

To convince her superiors, Hopper resorted to a rather sly trick. She modified the compiler, then called B-0, to respond to instructions not only in English but in French and German as well. As she later explained, "If you do something once, it's an accident; if you do it twice it's a coincidence; but if you do it three times, you've uncovered a natural law!"

Shortly after her trilingual demonstration, the compiler, named FLOW-MATIC by the sales department, was released to the public, to join MATH-MATIC, Speedcoding and other laborsaving languages. Thus, by the middle of the 1950s, with computer usage growing exponentially, a sturdy foundation was in place, and the golden age of language development was about to begin.

A Language on Intimate Terms with the Machine

Writing instructions for a computer in the strings of binary digits that constitute the machine's primary language can be an excruciating task. To get a computer to execute any one of the more than 200 fundamental operations it can perform, the programmer must remember or look up the unique code of zeros and ones required to set that particular operation in motion. In addition, the programmer must keep track of the address in the computer's memory — a numbered location, also written in zeros and ones — where each piece of the program's data is stored. And to complicate matters even further, the codes for both instructions and addresses vary according to the make and model of the machine for which the program is written.

Assembly language offers programmers a first step away from the binary minutiae by employing symbols that are more easily understood and remembered. These symbols may take the form of terms, such as LOAD or ADD, that represent the computer's core operations. Similarly, the information to be manipulated may be represented by symbolic names, chosen by the programmer; in effect, these names stand for the memory addresses where the information will be stored. A programmer writing in assembly language groups these terms and names into multiple combinations of computer operations, thus enabling the machine to carry out the many tasks that make up even a short program. Before the program can be run, however, it must be translated into zeros and ones for the benefit of the machine. The computer itself performs this conversion, using a separate program called an assembler.

Though far less complex than any real computer, the schematic machine shown on the following pages, together with its assembly language, serves to illustrate the intimate relationship between a computer's hardware and the terms and symbolic names of an assembly-language program. This simple example also demonstrates some of the basic principles that programmers in such a language must master to harness the full power of their machines.

The Basic Elements of Memory and Processor

In its simplest form, a computer has two main components: a memory, where information is stored, and a central processing unit (CPU), where it is manipulated. A third element, the clock, coordinates the electronic activities involved in transferring the information to and from memory and in working on it in the CPU.

A computer's memory consists of an arrangement of storage areas that hold information represented by the ones and zeros of the machine's language. To give the computer a way to keep track of this information and retrieve it when necessary, each storage area is identified by a binary address. In writing an assembly-language program, however, the programmer uses easy-to-remember symbolic names to represent this information; FIRSTNUM, for example, might designate the first number in an addition operation. Before the program is run, the assembler—the software that converts assembly language to machine code—figures out where in memory the information will be stored.

Information in memory includes both data and the instructions for processing the data once it has been moved into the CPU. In the simplified computer shown at right and on the pages that follow, the CPU has several working areas called registers, which temporarily store instructions, data and memory addresses during processing. Another part of the CPU, the arithmetic logic unit (ALU), actually operates on the data. Here, the ALU can only add and subtract; in a real computer, the CPU has many more registers and an ALU capable of numerous logical and mathematical operations, allowing the machine to perform complex computations with fewer steps.

Both the memory and the CPU of a computer go through their paces in time to electronic pulses generated by the computer's clock. The clock is actually more like a metronome, keeping up a steady beat to coordinate the actions of all of the computer's components. In a modern computer, the speed of the clock is measured in millions of pulses per second, a rate of activity that allows the machine to execute complicated jobs at lightning speed.

As shown in the example at right, a computer operates by retrieving, or reading, data from memory, manipulating the data in the CPU, and returning, or writing, the results to memory. Here, the assembly-language instruction LOAD tells the CPU to read a value from an address in memory — represented by the name FIRSTNUM — and copy it into a register in the CPU. The ADD instruction reads a value from another memory address — here called SECONDNUM — and adds it to the first. Finally, the STORE instruction writes the result, SUM, into a memory address that will be associated with that name.

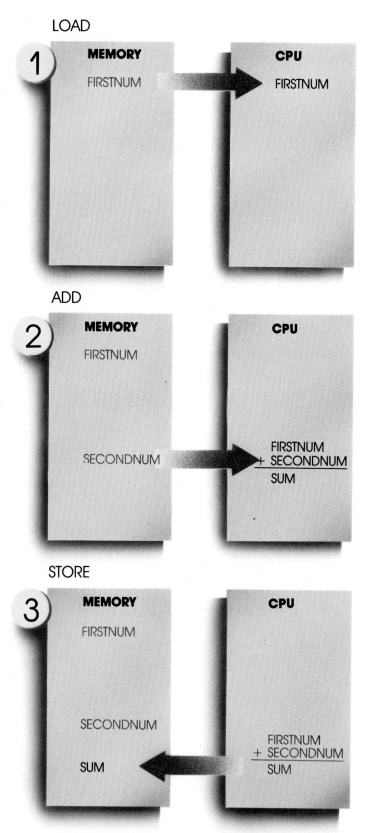

LOAD

1

MEMORY	CPU
FIRSTNUM	FIRSTNUM

ADD

2

MEMORY	CPU
FIRSTNUM	
SECONDNUM	FIRSTNUM + SECONDNUM / SUM

STORE

3

MEMORY	CPU
FIRSTNUM	
SECONDNUM	
SUM	FIRSTNUM + SECONDNUM / SUM

Each storage slot in a computer's memory has an address, represented in machine code by binary numbers (but shown here in decimal form for convenience). When information is written into a memory address, it replaces whatever was there. When information is read from an address, a copy is sent to the CPU or to another memory address, but the contents of the originating address remain unchanged.

The CPU divides its work among several elements. The program counter logs the address of the next instruction. The instruction decoder interprets an instruction for the CPU. The address decoder logs the address of the data to be operated on by that instruction. The accumulator holds data to be manipulated by the arithmetic and logic unit (ALU), as well as results of ALU manipulations. And the ALU performs addition and subtraction.

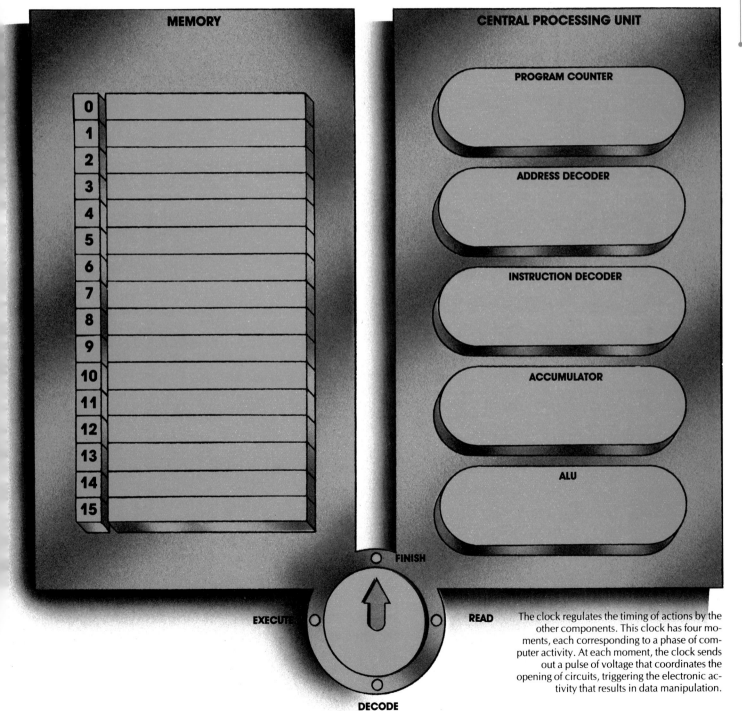

MEMORY

0
1
2
3
4
5
6
7
8
9
10
11
12
13
14
15

CENTRAL PROCESSING UNIT

PROGRAM COUNTER

ADDRESS DECODER

INSTRUCTION DECODER

ACCUMULATOR

ALU

FINISH

EXECUTE

READ

DECODE

The clock regulates the timing of actions by the other components. This clock has four moments, each corresponding to a phase of computer activity. At each moment, the clock sends out a pulse of voltage that coordinates the opening of circuits, triggering the electronic activity that results in data manipulation.

Fundamental Tasks in the Central Processor

Assembly-language instructions are made up of two parts, called the opcode and the operand. The opcode, for operation code, tells the computer what operation is to be performed; the operand is the symbolic name for the memory address of the data to be operated on, or in some cases, the

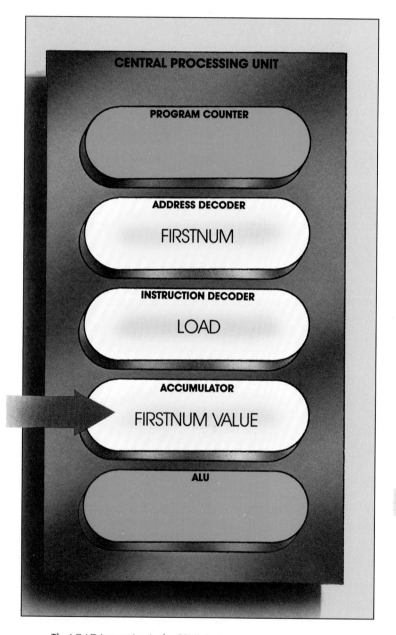

The LOAD instruction in the CPU's instruction decoder tells the CPU to read the value stored at the memory address indicated by the operand — in this case, the address labeled FIRSTNUM — and to write a copy of that value in the accumulator.

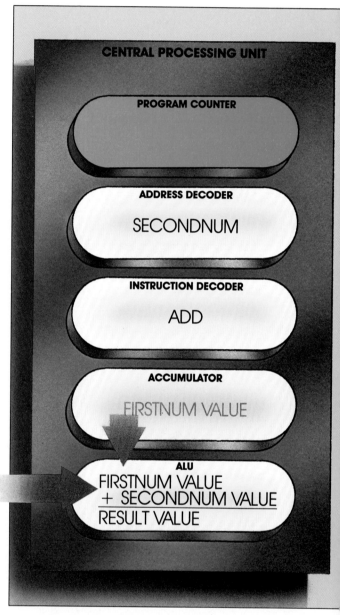

The ADD instruction is carried out in two steps. First, a number is brought into the ALU from the address indicated by the operand (here, labeled SECONDNUM) and is added, in the ALU (above), to the number from the accumulator; the result is then transferred from the ALU back into the accumulator (above, right), overwriting the value previously held there. (The instruction SUB is similar, except that the number read from the operand is subtracted from the number in the accumulator.)

address of another instruction. In the simple computer shown here, an instruction is read into the CPU from memory and goes first to the instruction decoder, which keeps the opcode and writes a copy of the operand into the address decoder. The instruction-decoder circuitry then converts the opcode into a series of electronic signals that will execute the command represented by the opcode. The address decoder responds to signals by opening the circuits along which data may travel either to the CPU from the memory address specified by the operand or from the CPU to that address.

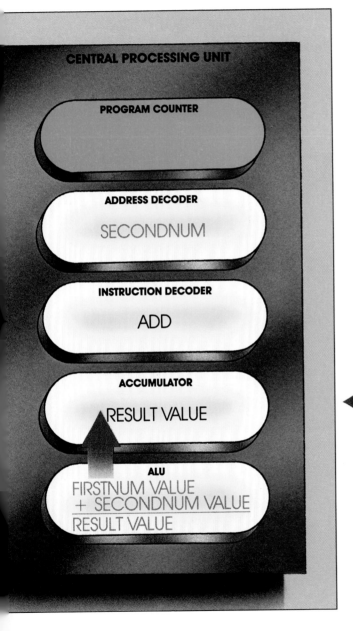

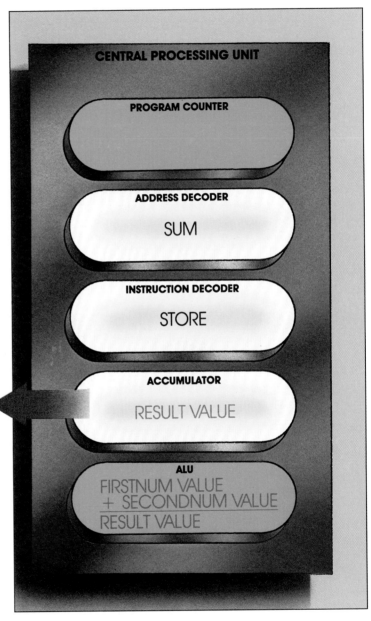

The STORE instruction sends the number in the accumulator back into memory — in this case, to the address labeled SUM. Any value previously stored at that memory location is overwritten by the new information.

The Recurring Phases of the Instruction Cycle

The operations initiated by an assembly-language instruction such as LOAD or STORE are actually the final phase of a series of activities called an instruction cycle. Although the computer performs a different set of operations to execute each of its instructions, the phases of the cycle are the same for all instructions. And in any computer, the purpose of the instruction cycle is the same: to read an instruction from memory, decode it, execute it, and prepare for the next instruction. In carrying out the sequence of instructions that makes up a program, a computer goes through its instruction cycle over and over again, sometimes for millions or even billions of repetitions.

In the schematic computer shown here, an assembly-language program has been translated by the assembler and stored in the computer's memory (for clarity, opcodes are

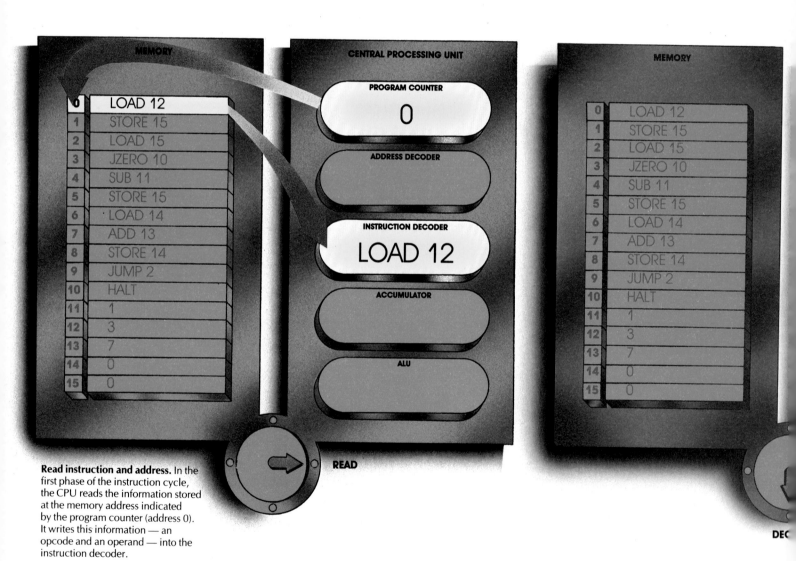

Read instruction and address. In the first phase of the instruction cycle, the CPU reads the information stored at the memory address indicated by the program counter (address 0). It writes this information — an opcode and an operand — into the instruction decoder.

shown as assembly-language terms rather than the binary numbers they would be at this point; similarly, operands, which would have been translated into binary memory addresses by now, are shown in decimal form for clarity). This computer has a four-phase cycle, each phase triggered by a clock pulse. In the first phase, the CPU reads the number in the program counter. Most computers are designed to reset the program counter to a particular number — representing a memory address — each time a program is run; a programmer can then be sure to store the first instruction of any program at the indicated address. Here, the initial setting for the program counter is 0; interpreting this number as a memory address, the computer copies the contents of that address into the instruction decoder.

In the second phase, the CPU decodes the full instruction,

copying the operand (that is, an address) into the address decoder and leaving the opcode (that is, an operational instruction) in the instruction decoder. In the third and fourth phases, the operations required to execute the instruction are performed. The operations for some instructions — LOAD and STORE, for example — can be performed in a single clock phase. Other instructions, such as ADD and SUB, take two phases to complete.

At the same time that it executes the instruction, the CPU automatically adds 1 to the number in the program counter. Thus, in the next instruction cycle, the CPU will copy the contents of the next memory address into the instruction decoder. In this way, the computer works its way sequentially through memory, performing each successive instruction of a program in turn.

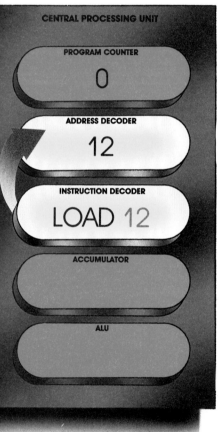

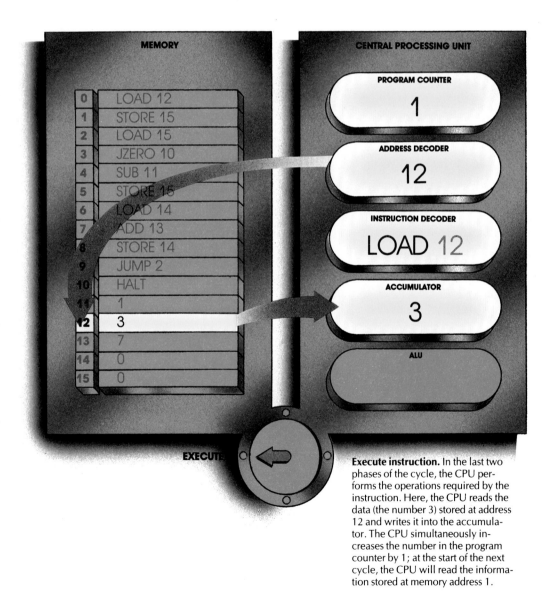

Transfer address. In the second phase, the CPU reads the operand (12) from the instruction decoder and writes it into the address decoder, leaving the opcode (LOAD) to be interpreted by the instruction decoder.

Execute instruction. In the last two phases of the cycle, the CPU performs the operations required by the instruction. Here, the CPU reads the data (the number 3) stored at address 12 and writes it into the accumulator. The CPU simultaneously increases the number in the program counter by 1; at the start of the next cycle, the CPU will read the information stored at memory address 1.

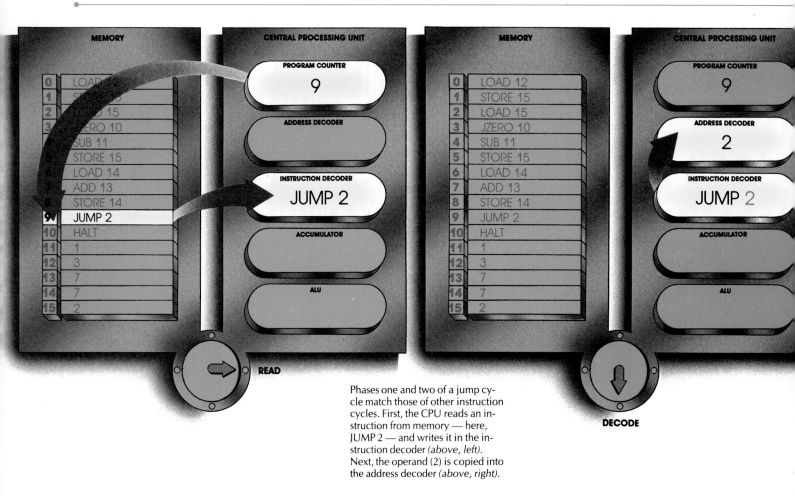

MEMORY

0	LOAD 12
1	S...
2	...D 15
3	...ERO 10
	SUB 11
	STORE 15
	LOAD 14
	ADD 13
	STORE 14
9	JUMP 2
10	HALT
11	1
12	3
13	7
14	7
15	2

CENTRAL PROCESSING UNIT

PROGRAM COUNTER
9

ADDRESS DECODER

INSTRUCTION DECODER
JUMP 2

ACCUMULATOR

ALU

READ

MEMORY

0	LOAD 12
1	STORE 15
2	LOAD 15
3	JZERO 10
4	SUB 11
5	STORE 15
6	LOAD 14
7	ADD 13
8	STORE 14
9	JUMP 2
10	HALT
11	1
12	3
13	7
14	7
15	2

CENTRAL PROCESSING UNIT

PROGRAM COUNTER
9

ADDRESS DECODER
2

INSTRUCTION DECODER
JUMP 2

ACCUMULATOR

ALU

DECODE

Phases one and two of a jump cycle match those of other instruction cycles. First, the CPU reads an instruction from memory — here, JUMP 2 — and writes it in the instruction decoder *(above, left)*. Next, the operand (2) is copied into the address decoder *(above, right)*.

Changing the Program Sequence

In the course of its normal operation, a computer executes the instructions of a program in strict sequential order. But the program can also be written to make the computer disregard that sequence. This is done by inserting a number into the program counter to cause the computer to commence its next instruction cycle at a memory address other than the one that would follow sequentially. Commands that effect this sort of break in the stated sequence of a program are known as jump or branch instructions.

A JUMP command is useful for getting the computer to repeat the execution of a long series of instructions; in a programming technique called a loop, the computer is simply told to go back to the first instruction of the series and begin its sequential count again. Alternatively, the computer can be told to bypass a series of instructions by re-starting its count at some point beyond the last instruction in the series.

The key to this flexibility is the program counter. Ordinarily, the number in the program counter is automatically increased by 1 during the last phase of an instruction cycle. The JUMP instruction overrides this process; when the instruction's opcode is executed, the address indicated by the operand is loaded into the program counter. Thus, when the next instruction cycle begins, the CPU reads the contents of a memory address that is dictated by the programmer, rather than the address that follows the JUMP instruction in the program listing. This capacity for changing the sequence in which instructions are executed allows a programmer to construct complex, multidimensional programs that can perform extremely sophisticated tasks.

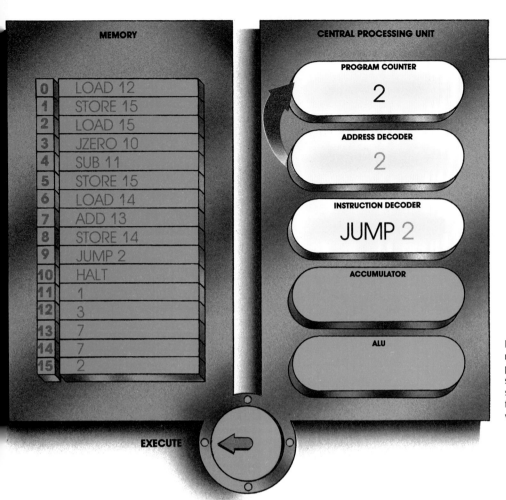

In the final phase of a JUMP command, the operand is copied into the program counter. This changes the sequential flow of the program; the instruction stored at the address specified by the program counter (LOAD 15) will now be performed next.

A JUMP That Looks before It Leaps

In some programs, the order in which the computer executes instructions needs to be altered only when a particular condition is met. The command that achieves this powerful flexibility is known as a conditional jump. It allows the course of the program to be controlled by intermediate results that occur as the program runs. Each time a conditional jump is invoked, the CPU examines the value held in a specified location, such as the accumulator or a special-purpose register. The jump is executed only if that value is identical to the one indicated by the instruction; if not, program instructions are followed in sequence.

With the JZERO command here, the CPU looks at the accumulator's contents. If the value there is 0, the operand in the address decoder is copied to the program counter and the jump occurs. If the value in the accumulator is not 0, the program counter is increased by 1, and sequential program flow continues.

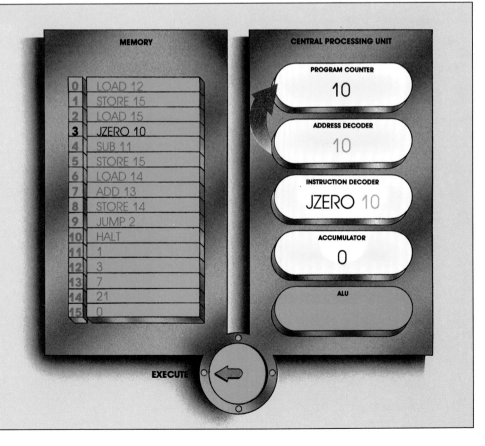

Changing Symbols into Machine Code

An assembly-language program is simply a list of instructions and other words that, when translated into binary machine code, trigger certain sequences of computer operations to carry out a particular task. The program shown on these pages does the simple job of multiplying two numbers; its instructions are organized so that the multiplication is accomplished by repeated addition. The two numbers to be multiplied are, in effect, operands — here called MPLIER and MPLICAND — and the result is called SUM. All operands are given initial values before the original program, or source code, is translated. Thus, the program used here to multiply 3 times 7 could also be used to multiply any two numbers, simply by changing the initial values of MPLIER and MPLICAND.

The program, shown in its original form below, contains not only opcodes, operational instructions represented by assembly-language terms, and operands, symbolic names representing memory addresses, but also another set of symbolic names known as labels (below, brown). Labels correspond to the symbolic names used as operands, marking lines in the program that contain information intended for use as an operand. For example, the label MPLICAND marks the line in the program containing the numeric value 7; MPLICAND is also the symbolic name for the operand in the instruction LOAD MPLICAND. Similarly, the label LOOP marks the line in the program that is the beginning of a loop; LOOP is also the symbolic name for the operand in the instruction JUMP LOOP. The assembler, the program that converts the assembly-language program into machine code, uses the labels during translation to associate operands with the appropriate data values or instructions. As illustrated at right, the assembler generally does its work in two passes through the source code.

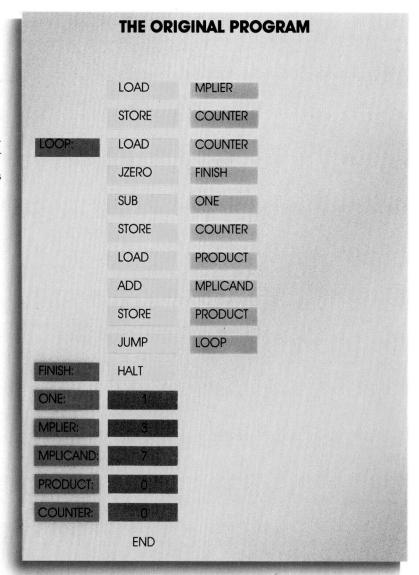

THE ORIGINAL PROGRAM

Opcodes (yellow) represent the actions that the CPU can perform. These include moving data from place to place (LOAD and STORE), operating on the data (ADD and SUB), changing the flow of the program (JUMP and JZERO), and causing the computer to stop (HALT). Each opcode except HALT requires an operand that tells the CPU the address of the data to be used in executing the instruction.

Operands (purple) represent memory addresses and are also references to labels marking other lines in the program. Operands such as LOOP and FINISH may indicate the destination of a jump instruction, that destination being a line containing another instruction; others, such as COUNTER and PRODUCT, may refer to lines in the program where data values are to be found.

	LOAD	MPLIER
	STORE	COUNTER
LOOP:	LOAD	COUNTER
	JZERO	FINISH
	SUB	ONE
	STORE	COUNTER
	LOAD	PRODUCT
	ADD	MPLICAND
	STORE	PRODUCT
	JUMP	LOOP
FINISH:	HALT	
ONE:	1	
MPLIER:	3	
MPLICAND:	7	
PRODUCT:	0	
COUNTER:	0	

END

Labels (brown) indicate lines in the program associated with operands. These lines may contain another instruction, as in the case of LOOP and FINISH, or values to be put into memory at locations determined by the assembler. ONE, MPLIER, MPLICAND, PRODUCT and COUNTER are all labels for values.

Data (red) are the actual values used when the program is run. Some values are fixed, as in the case of ONE. Other values, such as MPLIER and MPLICAND, must be changed if the program is used to multiply different numbers; here they are set to 3 and 7. The values in PRODUCT and COUNTER start at 0 but will change as the program runs. In the assembly-language program, these data are written in decimal form; they are converted to binary by the assembler.

NUMBERING THE LINES

	LOAD	MPLIER	0
	STORE	COUNTER	1
LOOP:	LOAD	COUNTER	2
	JZERO	FINISH	3
	SUB	ONE	4
	STORE	COUNTER	5
	LOAD	PRODUCT	6
	ADD	MPLICAND	7
	STORE	PRODUCT	8
	JUMP	LOOP	9
FINISH:	HALT		10
ONE:	1		11
MPLIER:	3		12
MPLICAND:	7		13
PRODUCT:	0		14
COUNTER:	0		15
	END		

First pass. The assembler reads the entire program, stopping after the word END. It counts the lines of the program (left) and assigns a binary memory address to each line (shown here in decimal for clarity). The assembler also creates a symbol table in memory (below), where each label is listed the first time it appears.

SYMBOL TABLE

SYMBOL	LINE	BINARY ADDRESS
LOOP	2	0000 0010
FINISH	10	0000 1010
ONE	11	0000 1011
MPLIER	12	0000 1100
MPLICAND	13	0000 1101
PRODUCT	14	0000 1110
COUNTER	15	0000 1111

INSTRUCTION TABLE

OPCODE	BINARY EQUIVALENT
LOAD	1000 0000
STORE	1010 0000
ADD	0110 0000
SUB	0100 0000
JUMP	1110 0000
JZERO	1100 0000
HALT	0000 0000

The tables. After the first pass, the assembler completes the symbol table (top), filling in for each label the binary memory address assigned to that label's program line. During final translation, the assembler will refer to the symbol table and to a permanent instruction table (above), which contains the binary form of each opcode.

GENERATING MACHINE CODE

	LOAD	MPLIER	0	1000 0000	0000 1100
	STORE	COUNTER	1	1010 0000	0000 1111
LOOP:	LOAD	COUNTER	2	1000 0000	0000 1111
	JZERO	FINISH	3	1100 0000	0000 1010
	SUB	ONE	4	0100 0000	0000 1011
	STORE	COUNTER	5	1010 0000	0000 1111
	LOAD	PRODUCT	6	1000 0000	0000 1110
	ADD	MPLICAND	7	0110 0000	0000 1101
	STORE	PRODUCT	8	1010 0000	0000 1110
	JUMP	LOOP	9	1110 0000	0000 0010
FINISH:	HALT		10	0000 0000	
ONE:	1		11		0000 0001
MPLIER:	3		12		0000 0011
MPLICAND:	7		13		0000 0111
PRODUCT:	0		14		0000 0000
COUNTER:	0		15		0000 0000
	END				

Second pass. The assembler replaces opcodes with their binary forms, operands with their binary memory addresses, and decimal data values with their binary equivalents. The resulting machine-code version of the program is ready to be run on the computer.

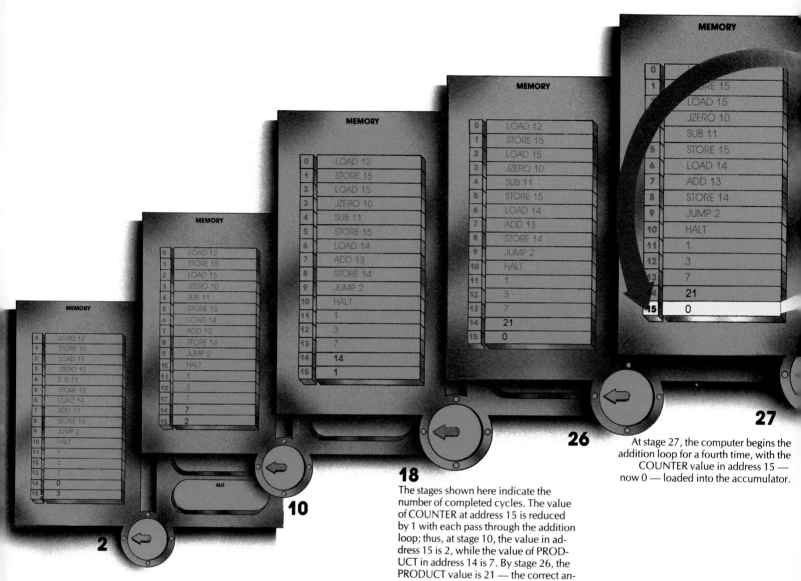

2

10

18
The stages shown here indicate the number of completed cycles. The value of COUNTER at address 15 is reduced by 1 with each pass through the addition loop; thus, at stage 10, the value in address 15 is 2, while the value of PRODUCT in address 14 is 7. By stage 26, the PRODUCT value is 21 — the correct answer — and the COUNTER value is 0.

26

27
At stage 27, the computer begins the addition loop for a fourth time, with the COUNTER value in address 15 — now 0 — loaded into the accumulator.

A Program in Action: Instructions at Work

The assembled program, now entirely in binary machine code, is electronically loaded into the computer's memory. This is done in such a way that when the machine is told to run a program, the first instruction it needs will be stored in the memory address that the CPU is designed to turn to first — in this case, address 0. Once the computer begins to perform instruction cycles, it continues until it reaches a HALT instruction, which tells it to stop executing program instructions and wait for further commands.

In running the program shown here (for clarity, memory addresses are in decimal form and instructions are still in assembly language), the computer begins by loading the value of MPLIER (at address 12), then storing that value as COUNTER. The value of COUNTER determines the number of times that the computer will perform the loop that begins with the instruction at address 2 and ends with the JUMP at address 9. Each time the computer goes through the loop, the subtraction instruction reduces the value in COUNTER by 1; when the value reaches 0, the JZERO at address 3 directs the computer to address 10, which contains the HALT instruction.

On each pass through the loop, the computer adds the value in MPLICAND to the current value of PRODUCT, which is 0 when the program begins. When the number in COUNTER reaches 0, the addition has been performed MPLIER times, and the final result is stored in PRODUCT.

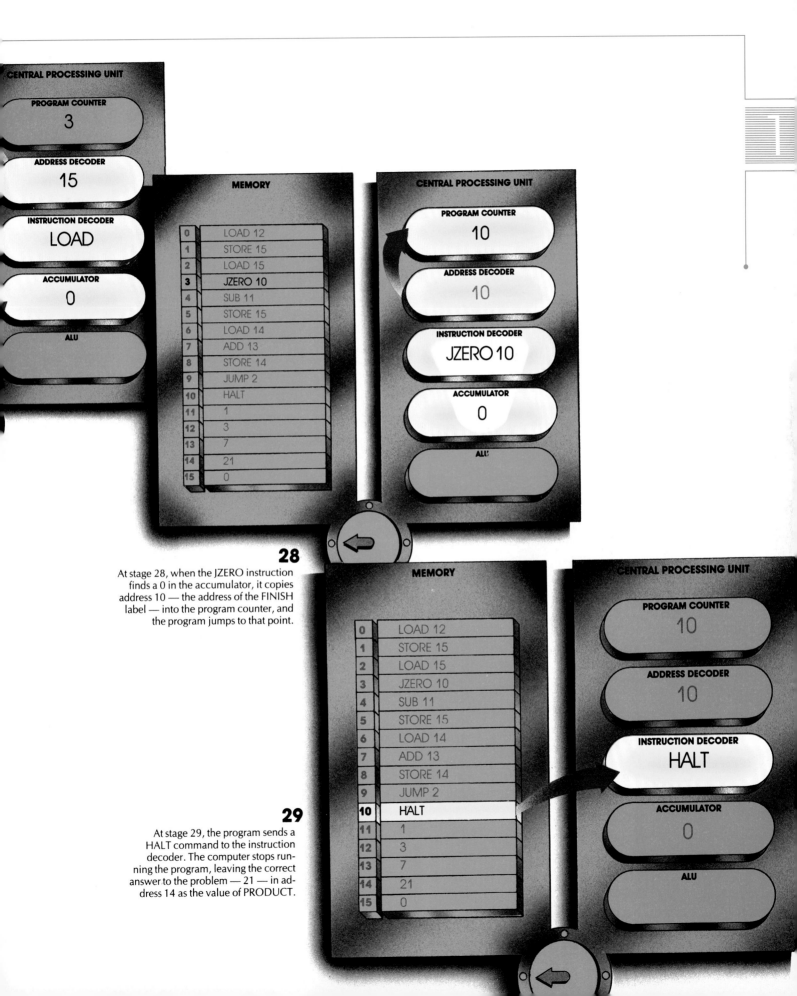

CENTRAL PROCESSING UNIT

PROGRAM COUNTER
3

ADDRESS DECODER
15

INSTRUCTION DECODER
LOAD

ACCUMULATOR
0

ALU

MEMORY

0	LOAD 12
1	STORE 15
2	LOAD 15
3	JZERO 10
4	SUB 11
5	STORE 15
6	LOAD 14
7	ADD 13
8	STORE 14
9	JUMP 2
10	HALT
11	1
12	3
13	7
14	21
15	0

CENTRAL PROCESSING UNIT

PROGRAM COUNTER
10

ADDRESS DECODER
10

INSTRUCTION DECODER
JZERO 10

ACCUMULATOR
0

ALU

28

At stage 28, when the JZERO instruction finds a 0 in the accumulator, it copies address 10 — the address of the FINISH label — into the program counter, and the program jumps to that point.

MEMORY

0	LOAD 12
1	STORE 15
2	LOAD 15
3	JZERO 10
4	SUB 11
5	STORE 15
6	LOAD 14
7	ADD 13
8	STORE 14
9	JUMP 2
10	HALT
11	1
12	3
13	7
14	21
15	0

CENTRAL PROCESSING UNIT

PROGRAM COUNTER
10

ADDRESS DECODER
10

INSTRUCTION DECODER
HALT

ACCUMULATOR
0

ALU

29

At stage 29, the program sends a HALT command to the instruction decoder. The computer stops running the program, leaving the correct answer to the problem — 21 — in address 14 as the value of PRODUCT.

Three Commercial Giants

Late one Friday afternoon in April of 1957, the postman delivered a mysterious package to the computer center at the Westinghouse-Bettis Atomic Power Laboratory near Pittsburgh. Programmer Herb Bright and a couple of his colleagues, with most of the week's work behind them, were loitering in a hallway just outside the room housing their sleek new IBM 704. Out of curiosity, they opened the unlabeled box. It contained about 2,000 punched computer cards, but no instructions or explanation of any kind.

Bright had a hunch about the cards; something interesting, he knew, was going on at IBM. For months now, the big computer company had been cleaning the bugs out of a high-level language intended for use on the 704. Called FORTRAN, for Mathematical Formula Translating System, it was an automatic coding system designed to take some of the drudgery out of programming. Was it possible the postman had brought the long-awaited FORTRAN compiler, the software necessary for translating FORTRAN programs into machine code? Itching with anticipation, Bright and his friends decided to load the mystery cards into the 704 and see what happened.

As the machine digested the information on the cards, its memory tapes turned and stopped, turned and stopped. When the tapes were still, the computer's ready light glowed. Bright fed a test program, written in FORTRAN, into the 704's reader and pressed the start button. The printer chattered. The new compiler had a message for its users; it had found an error in the program, a comma missing from a statement on card No. 25. The programmers were amazed at this precision: The error messages they were accustomed to seeing were cryptic numerical codes and were hard to track down. They corrected the offending statement and hit the start button again. The tapes started turning, and the computer produced a small deck of program cards. When these were fed into the reader, the printer started up and did not stop until it had filled 28 pages with output. The 704 had made a few minor format errors. "But the numbers were right! The numbers were right!" Bright exclaimed later. "Computing would never be the same."

Bright and his co-workers had just joined the ranks of the earliest users of FORTRAN, the first widely available high-level language. Its introduction was probably the most important milestone in the history of computer languages. Since that day in 1957, the number of programmers using — and occasionally abusing — FORTRAN has grown large enough to populate a fair-size city.

A generation later, FORTRAN has come to be considered something of a relic among computer languages. Programmers have called it — sometimes affectionately, but often otherwise — a "dinosaur," an "intellectual roadblock" and even a "collection of warts held together by bits of syntax." In the caustic opinion of software authority Edsger Dijkstra, teaching FORTRAN to computer-science students should be punishable as a capital offense. Nevertheless, decades after its origin, FORTRAN remains one of the most popular of all languages. Its capacity for manipulating numbers has earned it a vast following of scientists and engineers. Its ability to swallow and digest long strings of numbers, however, is only a

FORTRAN, COBOL and ALGOL effectively bridged the communications gap between programmer and machine in the late 1950s and have dominated the computing landscape ever since. Most of today's programs are written in languages that are variations on these three classics.

partial explanation for its remarkable staying power. Much of its longevity must be credited to the simple fact that FORTRAN was there first.

The researchers at IBM who created FORTRAN had no idea their language would have the enormous impact it did. When they began work early in 1954, computer science was a freewheeling, rough-and-ready affair. Years later, the team's chief, John Backus, recalled, "Recognition in the small programming fraternity was more likely to be accorded for a colorful personality, an extraordinary feat of coding, or the ability to hold a lot of liquor well than it was for an intellectual insight. Ideas flowed freely along with the liquor."

Programmers and computer scientists were a new breed. Their résumés were short. One IBM manager of the time decided that chess players made good programmers, so he interviewed prospects while watching them play a member of his staff — who happened to be the U.S. chess champion. Few of the eight men assigned to the FORTRAN project had more than a passing familiarity with computers. They were drawn from universities and from aircraft companies, as well as from IBM's own programming ranks. Even John Backus had only a few years' experience with computers when he launched the FORTRAN project.

Prior to his college days, Backus had been an indifferent student ("I was thrown out of more schools than I can remember"). After serving a hitch in the army during World War II, he drifted to New York City and enrolled in a school for radio technicians on the GI Bill. "My greatest ambition," he confessed later, "was to build a good hi-fi set." But an instructor at the school who taught radio/TV repair kindled Backus' interest in the potential joys of mathematics and encouraged him to continue his studies at Columbia University. In this mod-

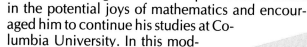

est fashion began one of the most creative careers in computer history.

Backus was 25 years old, with the ink barely dry on his master's degree in mathematics from Columbia, when he joined IBM as a programmer in 1950. Before long, he was leading the team that developed the interpreter called Speed-coding, used on the IBM 701. Then he turned his hand to hardware design, as part of the team that was building a more powerful successor to the 701, the IBM 704. Late in 1953, Backus, who contends that he has "always been a lazy person," approached his boss with a laborsaving suggestion: a sophisticated language and compiler to make programming the new 704 a less onerous task. His system would allow the user to write programs in algebraic notation. The compiler would translate this notation into machine code automatically.

Backus' suggestion came at a good time. After a late start, IBM was pushing hard to increase its computer sales. To this end, the company supported programs in computer science at Columbia, Harvard and several other universities. But IBM was still looking for a way to bring down the high cost of programming and make computers less intimidating — in effect, "friendlier" — to their users. Most scientists, engineers and educators had neither the time nor the patience to use machine code or even assembly language, which required a reasonably intimate knowledge of how the computer itself worked. But they might be persuaded to learn a high-level language, especially if it resembled familiar algebraic formulas. Backus was given the green light.

FORTRAN's birthplace was the IBM world-headquarters building on Madison Avenue in New York City. Backus' group settled into offices on the 19th floor, within earshot of the building's elevator machinery and surrounded by what might be described as an atmosphere of skepticism. Earlier attempts to improve on machine code and assembly language had in some cases been oversold as "almost human" means of communicating with computers, a claim that tended to foster disbelief. But the FORTRAN team pushed on. They structured their new language with basic notions such as assignment statements — $N = 100$, for example — that specified values for variables. They added subscripted variables, which told the computer which item in a list of variables was desired; for example, $X(3)$ meant the third item in the list called X. And they included the very important DO statement, which allowed looping, or repeating a series of instructions a number of times. According to Backus, most people "think FORTRAN's main contribution was to enable the programmer to write programs in algebraic formulas instead of machine language, but it wasn't." Instead, Backus has said, "what FORTRAN did primarily was to mechanize the organization of loops" — a device that became invaluable in scientific applications.

Work on the language itself went quickly. "We simply made up the language as we went along," Backus recalled. But developing a compiler was another matter. Backus realized that to allay the computer community's serious doubts about the worth of automatic programming, as writing programs in high-level languages was called, FORTRAN programs would have to be as fast and dependable as those written directly in machine code or assembly language.

Structuring an efficient and reliable FORTRAN compiler turned out to be far more challenging than had been imagined. The team had to concern itself with input, output, DO loops and the host of intricate steps necessary to transform high-level commands into machine code. Early plans called for the compiler to be completed within six months; in fact, six months remained the unchanging interval to completion for more than two years. Through the end of 1956 and into 1957, the pace of refining and debugging the compiler grew intense. Team members often rented rooms in a midtown hotel, where they slept by day, and then worked all night at the office to get in as much uninterrupted computer time as possible. One by one, the bugs were exterminated until, in April 1957, the compiler seemed ready for customers who had already leased the 704. Owing to what Backus described as a "vast confusion," the FORTRAN compiler was sent to Westinghouse-Bettis in punched-card form, without instructions. This set the stage for Herb Bright's successful attempt to fly FORTRAN blind. Other users received the system on magnetic tape, along with an operator's manual.

Acceptance was grudging at first. As Backus recalled, programmers "were extremely skeptical about all of our claims." But compared with its predecessors, FORTRAN was relatively easy to learn and use. And IBM was providing the system without additional charge for use on the 704. As a result, by 1958 more than half the machine instructions at some 60 IBM computer installations nationwide were being produced automatically by FORTRAN instead of by hand.

Backus and his team anticipated that the success of FORTRAN would prompt other manufacturers to develop similar languages for their own machines, and eventually they did. But FORTRAN rapidly became a norm, adapted to a wide variety of computers. The first adaptation took place at IBM itself. A small team that included David Hemmes, a newcomer to IBM with a passion for racing hot rods in his spare time, set out to make FORTRAN compatible with the IBM 650, a smaller machine than the 704. Hemmes and his colleagues developed a system they dubbed FOR TRANSIT (later condensed to a single word). FORTRANSIT thus became the first major translator of source code (as high-level language programs are sometimes called) on more than one kind of computer. And within five years, FORTRAN was in use on half a dozen different IBM models, as well as on machines made by Sperry Rand, Philco and other manufacturers.

Not all of FORTRAN's sailing was so smooth. Early in 1957, while the debugging process was still going on, shortcomings in the language were already apparent. Backus and his designers saw the need for an even clearer diagnosis of program errors and a similar need for the use of subroutines, program sections that can be separately prepared and used repeatedly. This gave rise, only about a year after the release of the original, to FORTRAN II. Among other improvements, FORTRAN II allowed for links to assembly-language programs, so that programmers could, if they wished, write their programs partly in assembly and partly in FORTRAN. Later versions — FORTRAN III was written in 1958 and FORTRAN IV was announced in 1962 — further expanded FORTRAN's capabilities.

The heart of the language, its central statements and expressions, remained largely untouched over the years. But as FORTRAN was repeatedly adapted to run on systems for which it had not been designed, changes crept in. Tinkerers

At the age of 28, mathematician John Backus recruited and led the young IBM programming team that created FORTRAN. Released in 1957 after three years of development, FORTRAN was the first major high-level language.

dropped some features and added others. This led inevitably to confusion over what was and what was not legal in FORTRAN. For example, not all compilers handled the important DO loop in the same way. Some always executed the loop once before checking whether it should be executed at all. Others checked before executing. To tidy up the FORTRAN house, computer manufacturers and users agreed to a standardization of the language in 1966 and again in 1977.

FORTRAN is still a popular tool for programming, particularly among scientists. Most subsequent languages are either its direct or indirect descendants. But much of its historical significance lies in the fact that it was the first widely distributed commercial language. As an IBM manual in 1957 claimed, FORTRAN "provided an efficient means of writing 704 programs requiring no knowledge of the computer and a relatively short period of training." Henceforth, scientists, engineers and students could communicate with computers without depending on professional assembly-language programmers as intermediaries.

BUSINESS COMES TO COMPUTERS

Even as FORTRAN gained adherents in the traditional computer domains of science and engineering, the business world was making increasing demands on computing. Large corporations—which live by the formula that time equals money—recognized the profitable potential in computers that could process huge quantities of data at high speed. A few programming languages had in fact been created with business applications in mind. Prominent among them were FLOW-MATIC, which Grace Hopper had developed for Sperry Rand; an IBM business language called Commercial Translator; and the Air Force's AIMACO (from Air Matériel Command). But none of these early languages showed any promise of general acceptance, and none could function in more than one family of computers, a drawback true of many other languages appearing at this time.

Just as the Backus team at IBM had predicted, the appearance of FORTRAN set off a flurry of imitators. But most of these systems were not portable; they were specific to the computer for which they were designed. Since large organizations often dealt with more than one supplier, an increasing portability problem emerged. To keep up with the different languages, harried business programmers were forced to become polyglots. At one point, the Southern Railway Company had three kinds of computer, three separate computer centers, three programming staffs and one large efficiency problem. It was no way to run a railroad.

In April 1959, two years after the official launch of FORTRAN, an assortment of concerned users, manufacturers and academics held what amounted to a council of war at the University of Pennsylvania, one of the cradles of computer science. This small band quickly agreed that what it—and the world—needed was a standardized, machine-independent business language.

FORTRAN clearly was not the answer. Businesses were interested in handling payrolls faster and creating accessible lists of potential customers, not in solving equations. They needed a language that not only would permit such essential operations as sorting items in a data file, merging data files and generating usable reports, but would be as much like spoken English as possible.

Having little faith that any one computer company could be objective in such an undertaking, the group began seeking a neutral sponsor for the project. A small delegation headed by Grace Hopper approached the Department of Defense. Hopper had reason to believe the Pentagon would be interested in a highly portable business language. By 1959, DOD already had a regiment of computers, no fewer than 1,046 of them, of every available size and type. It was costing the government nearly $500 million a year to keep the disparate machines running and to program them in an ever-increasing number of languages. DOD shared the concern of many computer companies that a single manufacturer might soon corner the market. If that happened, DOD and other major users would be forced to deal with only one supplier. Most manufacturers were more than willing to help the Pentagon see to it that the market remained open.

THE BIRTH OF CODASYL

Responding with unusual alacrity to the Hopper delegation's overture, the Defense Department organized a special conference on computer languages, which met during the last week of May 1959 and was chaired by Charles Phillips, DOD's blunt-spoken director of Data Systems Research. The meeting would later be called CODASYL, for Conference on Data Systems Languages. Important suppliers such as Honeywell, General Electric, Burroughs, National Cash Register, Philco, Sperry Rand, Radio Corporation of America, Sylvania Electric Products and IBM sent representatives. Phillips told them that the Pentagon wanted a uniform programming language and wanted it soon.

The conferees responded to the challenge, as computer people often do, by dividing the problem into steps and tackling it by the numbers. They formed committees: A short-range task group would draw up a basic design; an intermediate-range group would use those specifications to fashion a workable programming system; and a long-range group would, over a period of years, develop what the CODASYL members hoped would be the last word in computer languages. A CODASYL Executive Committee, also chaired by Phillips, would oversee the whole process. As events turned out, however, the long-range committee never existed except as an empty box on an organization chart, the intermediate-range committee accomplished little, and the short-range committee ended up doing most of the work of creating the new language.

"It was by no means clear then that we were to do anything except try and combine the three known [business] languages of the time," said Jean Sammet, a Sylvania representative and a key member of the short-range committee. Sammet's group was to come up with a temporary solution, something that would give the intermediate-range group time to construct a more sophisticated product. So the short-range committee made an attempt to fit together major pieces of FLOW-MATIC, AIMACO and Commercial Translator. The pieces would not mesh. But after a summer of hard labor, several committee members felt they could build on these earlier languages and create one with an identity all its own.

At this point, the political difficulties of the committee structure became evident. The representatives of IBM took a forceful stand: Any attempt to write a wholly new language would carry the short-range task group dangerously beyond its mandate. Most of the committee, including its chairman, Joseph Wegstein of the National Bureau of Standards, disagreed. Wegstein rather grandly compared the committee's work to that of the Constitutional Convention of 1787. If those delegates had not gone beyond their original charter, he argued,

David Hemmes, an early computer-language designer, sits behind the wheel of his souped-up 1928 Model A at the Westhampton, New York, drag strip in 1957. Working as a programmer for IBM, Hemmes divided his time that summer between racing cars and writing FORTRANSIT, the first translator program that allowed small university computers to run programs written in FORTRAN.

"we would not have a Constitution." Despite the uncertainty about the short-range committee's role and apparent attempts to scuttle its efforts, the committee pushed ahead. By midautumn the new language had a definite shape and even a name. It was called Common Business Oriented Language, or COBOL. But the political struggle over its creation had only begun.

Events had caught members of the intermediate-range committee off guard. They had assumed that they, not the short-range committee, would design the new language. In October, they met and surprised everyone by passing a resolution that endorsed an entirely different language: FACT (Fully Automatic Compiling Technique), an innovative data-processing language that for months had been quietly under development at Honeywell. The specifications for FACT included several attractive features, such as data entry via cards and an easy-to-use report writer. The resolution called on the CODASYL Executive Committee to replace the COBOL specifications with those of FACT. Naturally, this outraged members of the short-range group, especially Jean Sammet, who had fought hard for the development of COBOL. According to Sammet, the Honeywell representative on her committee had been "remarkably silent" about the existence of FACT. "As can be imagined," Sammet wrote later, the resolution "had the effect of a major bombing on the short-range committee."

The behind-the-scenes tug of war that ensued continued until the next meeting of the Executive Committee. Feelings on both sides of the issue ran high. Unwilling to concede such a marketing advantage to Honeywell, most of the other companies lined up against FACT, and their wishes prevailed. When the Executive Committee convened in January 1960, it simply did not vote on the FACT resolution. The issue was raised at a later meeting, but by that time the committee had already approved the COBOL specifications.

Thus COBOL survived another attempt to bury it. Had a grave marker been needed, CODASYL chairman Charles Phillips already had one on hand. Sometime prior to the January meeting, a heavy crate had been delivered to Phillips' office. Inside, he found a small marble tablet with a recumbent lamb at the top. Chiseled into the stone was the word "COBOL." There was no epitaph.

Numerous epitaphs have been written since for COBOL, all of them premature. Now more than a quarter of a century old, the language is far from dead. By the end of the 1980s, COBOL programs worth well over $50 billion were running on business mainframes, an investment that virtually guarantees the language's perpetuation. Companies are reluctant to undertake additional costs by switching to a new system, even though the new one might prove more efficient in the long run. Moreover, COBOL has been updated regularly and is still very good at the job it was made for: processing business data.

The American business community took to COBOL almost from the start. Specifications for COBOL were published in April 1960, and by the end of that year, RCA and Sperry Rand were marketing their own COBOL compilers. Other manufacturers hurried to do the same. Conspicuously absent from the early rush to COBOL were IBM, which continued to promote Commercial Translator, and Honeywell, which had been stung by the FACT controversy. Eventually, even these holdouts made COBOL available to their customers, and the language quickly eclipsed both FACT and Commercial Translator.

The popularity of COBOL increased after the release of a new version in 1962. More powerful than its predecessor, the revised COBOL included a report writer and made use of the SORT verb. Interestingly, these features had been strong points of FACT. Many subsequent versions of COBOL have been approved by the watchdog CODASYL committee, which was not disbanded and has continued to meet regularly. As the number of data-processing departments using COBOL grew through the 1960s, a computer journal compared the language to crab grass: Despite attempts to root it out, it kept springing up and spreading.

COBOL serves business well for several reasons. The language is particularly effective at applying simple processes—addition, subtraction and the figuring of percentages, for example—to very large data files. It is also machine-independent; programs written in COBOL may be moved from one computer to another. And because COBOL employs ordinary English words and syntax, executives and managers unfamiliar with programming often can understand the code. (In a typical program, the computer may be instructed as follows: IF SALARY IS GREATER THAN 1000, PERFORM CHECK-SALARY-ROUTINE.) This readability also makes it easier to find bugs, add or change features and perform other standard maintenance functions. Indeed, well-maintained COBOL programs have been known to outlast the machines they run on.

Created to handle filing operations on masses of data, COBOL is not, as it turns out, a very good general-purpose language. Many mathematical and scientific programmers, the aristocrats of computer society, consider it verbose and cumbersome; like FORTRAN, it is often labeled a dinosaur. Yet COBOL's employment on a vast scale continues. Worldwide, about two thirds of the business code developed for mainframe computers is still being written in COBOL. The universal appeal of the language was clearly brought home to Grace Hopper when she was left behind after a tour of a computer center in Japan. She and her hosts could not understand one another until Hopper remembered some COBOL commands. "MOVE," she said, pointing to herself. "GOTO Osaka Hotel." The Japanese understood immediately and delivered her to her lodging.

Even before the advent of COBOL, a third attempt to create a universal computer language was under way. ALGOL, for Algorithmic Language, was an

To express his frustration over COBOL's initial lack of progress, one member of the design team — Howard Bromberg of RCA — mailed this tombstone to committee chairman Charles Phillips in early 1960. The group's design-by-consensus philosophy often tried the patience of team members, but by the end of the year, the strategy had produced the first version of the language that remains the international standard for business computing. (Bromberg finally confessed to his deed in 1985 — at COBOL's 25th anniversary celebration.)

algebraic language like FORTRAN, designed primarily for writing programs to solve numerical problems. Like COBOL, it was born in smoke-hazed committee rooms, the child of confrontation and compromise. But there the similarities stop. After years of wrangling, the ALGOL committees gave the world a language that attracted more interest than it did users. ALGOL was perhaps the first language that could accurately be called elegant, a term that Grace Hopper has defined as "like a great poem, simple and clear from a mathematical point of view, but not necessarily practical."

A GATHERING IN ZURICH

The impetus for ALGOL came from the introduction and rapid spread of FORTRAN in 1957. The computer community in Europe feared domination by IBM and other aggressive American firms; in the United States, meanwhile, programmers were anxious to establish a universal language for scientific programming. This widespread anxiety spawned an international summit. Talks began at the Swiss Federal Technical University, in Zurich, on May 27, 1958. When this first meeting adjourned little more than a week later, the entity that would be known as ALGOL 58 had come into being. Around the table at Zurich were gathered eight of the most respected names in computing, four each from Europe and the United States. John Backus, the father of FORTRAN, was there, as was Joe Wegstein, who later would chair the COBOL short-range committee.

The conference took as its motto the words of Voltaire: "The best is the enemy of the good" — meaning, do not delay the work forever by trying to make it perfect. Even so, progress was hard to achieve. The Americans argued for a language that would lend itself to workable compiler systems. The Europeans were less interested in compilers than in the power of the language to solve complex mathematical problems. On the second day, the talks almost broke down over a small but emotional issue: decimal points. One of the Europeans pounded on the table and shouted: "No! I will never use a period for a decimal point." The Americans, on the other hand, had nothing but disdain for the European notion of using a comma as a decimal point. That night, the tireless Wegstein trudged from room to room trying to calm the decimal-point tempest.

Wegstein's eventual solution to the problem provided the new language with one of its more remarkable features. ALGOL would be divided into three levels: a reference language to define each of ALGOL's concepts, publication languages to permit programs to be written and discussed, and hardware languages to allow the programs to be implemented on working computers. Because the Zurich negotiators would be discussing only the reference language and not the details of the publication and hardware languages, they could avoid making decisions about little things such as commas and periods.

The language created by the Zurich conference owed much to FORTRAN. In ALGOL, basic FORTRAN concepts were shuffled into a more logical — some would say more graceful — structure. But time restrictions and the need for compromise left many omissions. One of these was the absence of any procedure for the input and output of data. The ALGOL conferees had purposely not tackled this very machine-specific activity, assuming that those who chose to implement the language would write their own input/output programs. When the conference ended, some delegates went home believing the language was still far from

Multilingual Computing

Given the dominance of American technology during the first decades of the computer age, it is perhaps not surprising that virtually every high-level computer language since the groundbreaking appearance of FORTRAN in 1957 has employed sequences of letters that resemble English words. To-day, the French programmer assembling data to *fait un dump* onto *le floppy,* the German sitting at a *Mikrocomputer,* and the Japanese writing a new piece of *sofdo* are all likely to be conversing with their machines in English. Typically, they use the approach demonstrated in the Spanish program below, left, combining English keywords with variables and comments written in their own languages.

Although this type of mixed-language programming works, it imposes uncomfortable restraints on anyone who is not fluent in English. Depending on the complexity of the computer language, the programmer must learn anywhere from 80 to 200 or more essentially foreign words, impeding the dialogue between human and machine that computer lan-

```
10   ' Compra de divisas
20   PRINT "Qué es la tasa de cambio de pesetas a dólares?"
30   INPUT DOLARES
40   PRINT "Qué es la tasa de cambio de pesetas a francos suizos?"
50   INPUT FRANCOSSUIZOS
60   PRINT "Cuántas pesetas quieres cambiar?"
70   INPUT PESETAS
80   PRINT "Quieres cambiar a dólares (1) o a francos suizos (2)?"
90   PRINT "Contesta 1 o 2."
100  INPUT CONTESTAR
110  IF CONTESTAR = 2 THEN GOTO 150
120  LET NUMERO = PESETAS/DOLARES
130  PRINT PESETAS; "pesetas equivalen a"; NUMERO; "dólares."
140  END
150  LET NUMERO = PESETAS/FRANCOSSUIZOS
160  PRINT PESETAS; "pesetas equivalen a"; NUMERO; "francos suizos."
170  END
```

A simple foreign currency exchange program, written in BASIC, uses English-based keywords, such as PRINT, INPUT and GOTO, in conjunction with Spanish variables. The program asks for the rate of exchange between Spanish pesetas and American dollars *(line 20)* and between pesetas and Swiss francs *(line 40),* then asks whether the user wants to exchange pesetas for (1) dollars or (2) francs *(line 80).* Depending on the answer, the program will GOTO line 120 to compute the number of dollars a given number of pesetas will buy, or to line 150 to compute the number of francs.

```
1    * JOUR DE NOEL VERSION 3
2    *
5    CHAINE CODE
6    CODE ← '1LUNDI2MARDI3MERCREDI4JEUDI5VENDREDI6SAMEDI0DIMANCHE'
9    *
10   AFFICHER 'EN'; LIRE AN
20     SI AN ≥ 1900 ET AN < 2100 ALORS ALLER EN 40
21     AFFICHER 'MILLESIME INACCEPTABLE'; TERMINER
39   *
40       P ←AN − 1900
41       BIS ← ENT (P/4)
42       J ←2 + P + BIS
43       SEM ← ENT(J/7)
44       NOEL ← J − 7 * SEM
59   *
60   AFFICHER 'NOEL TOMBE UN', GRL(CODE,POS(CODE,1,CCA(NOEL)))
99   *
100  TERMINER
```

JOUR DE NOEL, a program written in the French computer language LSE, enables a user to find out on which of the seven days of the week — numbered and listed on line 6 — Christmas will fall in a given year. Much like BASIC, LSE numbers each line and uses simple keywords, such as *AFFICHER* (DIS-PLAY) and *TERMINER* (END), that a novice programmer can readily grasp. According to line 20, this particular program will only compute Christmas day for the years 1900 through 2100; otherwise, the program will *TERMINER* at line 21 with a message that the year is *INACCEPTABLE.*

guages are designed to promote. In some countries, programmers must also memorize the Roman alphabet — as perplexing to a Russian or Chinese computer user as Cyrillic characters or Oriental ideographs are to a Westerner.

In 1970, the French Ministry of National Education addressed the communications dilemma by sponsoring the development of LSE (for Langage Symbolique d'Enseignement, or Symbolic Teaching Language), which is derived solely from French words and syntax *(opposite, bottom)*. LSE is closely modeled on BASIC and is simple enough to be used by both adult nonprogrammers and schoolchildren. Taught in French schools since 1974, it has established itself as one of the few practical efforts to create and implement a computer language that does not use the English language as its base.

ALGOL 68 *(pages 76-78)*, designed in the late 1960s by an international committee of computer scientists, offers a broader solution to the problems facing non-English-speaking programmers. ALGOL 68 includes a feature that allows programmers to write algorithms employing specified keywords in their own language *(below)*. The keywords are contained in a translation table that is stored in the computer's memory and used by the ALGOL compiler to convert the program into machine code. Languages for which no translation tables exist may also be used for writing programs, but the algorithms must be translated by hand into one of the languages the compiler will accept before being fed into the computer.

```
menge datum = tupel (ganz tag, wort monat, ganz Jahr);
funktion naechster tag nach = (datum x) datum:
            wenn tag von x < monatslaenge (monat von x,  jahr von x)
            dann     (tag von x + 1,  monat von x,  jahr von x)
            wennaber monat von x = "Dezember"
            dann     (1,  "Januar",  jahr von x + 1)
            ansonsten (1,  nachfolgemonat (monat von x),  jahr von x)
            endewenn;
```

Three identical programs that compute the date that follows a given day, month and year are written in the respective Chinese, German and English variants of ALGOL 68. German and American programmers can enter their algorithms directly into the computer, accompanied by the appropriate translation table. The ideographs of the Chinese program, as with other programs written in a non-Roman alphabet, are first translated into the keywords contained in one of the Roman-alphabet translation tables (typically English) before the program is presented to the computer.

```
集合    日期 = 结构 (整形日, 字符形月, 整形年);
函数    下一天 = (日期 x) 日期:
            如果   日对于 x < 月的长度 (月对于 x, 年对于 x)
            那么   (日对于 x + 1, 月对于 x, 年对于 x)
            否则如果  月对于 x = "12月份"
            那么   (1, "1月份", 年对于 x + 1)
            否则   (1, 下一个月 (月对于 x, 年对于 x)
            条件结束,
```

```
mode date = struct (int day,  string month, int year);
proc the day following  = (date x) date:
            if day of x < length of month (month of x,  year of x)
            then (day of x + 1, month of x,  year of x)
            elif   month of x = "December"
            then (1, "January",  year of x + 1)
            else (1,  successor of month (month of x),  year of x)
            fi;
```

finished. But other conferees departed with high hopes that ALGOL was en route to becoming the longed-for international standard.

One of the optimists was John Backus. In February 1959, he presented ALGOL to SHARE, the powerful organization of IBM computer users, and generated an unexpected wave of enthusiasm. SHARE urged IBM to implement ALGOL. IBM responded by initiating a translator project, but the work proceeded lethargically. With FORTRAN gathering momentum, the world's leading marketer of computers could hardly be expected to throw its considerable weight behind a competing language. As months went by and the investment of SHARE's members in FORTRAN mounted, the users group began to back away from its early flirtation with ALGOL.

That did not stop Backus. Despite his employer's evident lack of interest, he continued to play a role in the development of ALGOL. After returning from Zurich, he became fascinated with syntax, the orderly arrangement of words and symbols that holds any language together; in computing, syntax determines if a program is grammatically correct. Backus created a rigorous and precise system for defining each term in a computer language in a logical way. For example, to define the term "digit," he wrote "<digit> := 0|1|2|3|4|5|6|7|8|9|." Soon programmers were referring to this approach to syntax as Backus Normal Form, or BNF. (A subsequent refinement of the work by the Danish astronomer Peter Naur led some to call it Backus Naur Form, but the acronym BNF remained the same.) BNF was to have a lasting influence on language design. It also laid the groundwork for a second round of discussions on ALGOL.

As problems with implementation grew and the promise of Zurich faded, the authors of ALGOL came to view their 1958 language as merely a draft. Clearly more work was needed. In January 1960, thirteen representatives from Europe and the United States, including seven of the original Zurich group, met in Paris to fill the holes left in ALGOL the first time around. One of the newcomers was Naur, who brought a proposed draft of a revised ALGOL written in BNF. Joe Wegstein, who served as chairman, wielded a firm gavel, but it has been said that the Paris conference produced only one unanimous decision: a vote to pose for a group photograph (right). Still, after eight days of tricky negotiations, the conferees left Paris in an optimistic mood, believing that a consensus had been reached and that even the most vocal critics of ALGOL would now be silenced. This proved not to be the case. Members of the American contingent had barely stepped off their plane when the new ALGOL 60 came under fire from within. A minority faction from the conference pointed to ambiguities remaining in the language and proceeded, uncharitably, to demonstrate them. Other critics complained that the language still had no input/output facilities.

TRANSATLANTIC DIVERGENCE

With SHARE now committed to FORTRAN, ALGOL 60 received a cool reception in America. Those who wanted to use it found it difficult to implement; even the most sophisticated computers of the time could not translate the full 116 characters in its reference-language character set. A few of the more romantically inclined members of the American community, however, looked at ALGOL and saw "an object of stunning beauty" — the poetic elegance that Grace Hopper described. They were not alone.

With rare unanimity, the ALGOL 60 design committee votes for a group photograph at the 1960 conference in Paris. On the committee were American computer scientist John Backus *(nearest the camera on right)* and Danish astronomer Peter Naur *(fourth from left)*, for whom Backus Naur Form, a notation system to describe computer languages, is named. John McCarthy, creator of LISP, snapped the picture.

The Europeans loved ALGOL. It allowed them to communicate powerful and complex ideas across borders and language barriers, and it freed the European computer industry from what had threatened to become utter reliance on American technology. Just as the U.S. Department of Defense lent crucial support to COBOL, the influential German Research Council and other European government agencies did the same for ALGOL. Energetic efforts to put ALGOL to work spread the language from Great Britain to the Soviet Union. Some of these attempts failed; for instance, an ambitious system in Britain was scrapped when programmers discovered that their ALGOL compiler could process only two characters per second. But most compilers proved highly successful, and ALGOL soon became the lingua franca of the European computer community.

Not so in the United States. Granted, ALGOL eventually found its way onto many American computers, but it never overcame the head start FORTRAN had gained in the marketplace. The less-than-vigorous support of American interests killed any possibility of ALGOL's evolving into the universal language that some had envisioned. Still, the theoretical impact of ALGOL was as significant in the United States as it was in Europe. The ALGOL 60 report became a testament for a generation of programmers and students of computer languages. "The ALGOL report is like the Bible," one computer scientist would comment later. "It's meant to be interpreted and not read or understood." Doctrinaire proponents of the language came to be known as ALGOL lawyers or even ALGOL theologians.

Over the years, a number of languages have been based at least in part on ALGOL, and its contributions to these languages include several major ideas. One of the most important is the concept of block structure, the dividing of programs into a number of self-contained units. Another is recursion, the ability of a program to refer to itself. A third, credited to Backus' BNF, is the formal definition of syntax, the precise way that words in the language are to be used. These and other fundamental concepts constitute the ALGOL legacy to computer-language designers.

IBM would take a careful look at that legacy when the computer colossus embarked on an ambitious language project late in 1963, in conjunction with the development of a new line of computers. Two years earlier, the company had realized that it needed to make a giant leap forward in technology if it wanted to maintain its market primacy. The result of that decision was the System/360, an impressive array of general-purpose computers. The machines were designed to handle with equal finesse the analytical computing needs of the scientific community and the data-processing needs of business, while filling the varied requirements of special-purpose users as well.

Naturally, these full-spectrum computers called for a powerful language to match. Inexplicably tardy in recognizing this, IBM had waited until six months before the scheduled unveiling of its new hardware to launch the language-development effort. SHARE, realizing its stake in the matter, helped IBM put together an Advanced Language Development Committee. This team, composed of SHARE representatives from Lockheed, Union Carbide and Standard Oil of California and including experts from IBM's own programming and language-design departments, would take on the challenge of creating the new language. IBM compiler specialist George Radin was named to head the project.

Time pressures haunted the team from the start. They began work in October 1963, and with the release of System/360 already scheduled for April 1964, they pushed hard to deliver on time. Enthusiasts of FORTRAN hoped to see their favorite language used as a blueprint. The committee eventually rejected FORTRAN; it was too restrictive to be the basis of a general-purpose language, but the debate delayed the project by several weeks. Starting over, the committee most often met on weekends, usually in hotel rooms in New York and Los Angeles. "At times," Radin said later, "the most vocal opponents of the activity were not FORTRAN advocates but neglected wives and husbands."

Despite management's urgings, specifications were not completed until February 1964. By then it was too late to include the new language in the elaborate preparations for System/360's April debut at 77 press conferences worldwide. Perhaps it was just as well. The committee effort, called the New Programming Language (and later PL/I for Programming Language One), was finally reported to SHARE in March. Some members panned it as formless, overcomplex and redundant. One compared it to "a 100-blade Swiss knife," and another asked sarcastically why the designers had left out the kitchen sink.

Hoping that implementation would clear up most of PL/I's problems, IBM put its laboratory in Hursley, England, to work on a compiler for it. The staff at Hursley found it needed a 200-page report to define the massive language. Hursley had to edit so heavily that members of the original design committee were barely able to identify the result as their handiwork. But the refinements had honed PL/I into a practical tool that many programmers welcomed when it was officially published, in December 1964.

IBM had hoped that PL/I would be the culmination of all that had been learned about languages in the previous decade. In some ways, it was. Many aspects of FORTRAN, COBOL and ALGOL were reflected in PL/I. But at the same time, critics contended that PL/I encompassed too much of what had come before it and served only to perpetuate the mistakes of the past. In the philosophical judgment of John Backus, the early commercial languages have had a negative impact on the development of PL/I and subsequent computer languages. Because these first high-level languages penetrated so deeply into the computing world, Backus has said, they stand to this day as roadblocks to superior languages and to a better understanding of computers themselves.

High-Level Tools for Shaping Solutions

Every high-level computer language is a compromise between the computer's requirement for precise, step-by-step instructions and the problem-solving needs of human programmers. Assembly languages *(pages 23-35)*, which are closely related to the operations of specific computers, require programmers to think in terms of the machine's central processing unit, numbered memory addresses, and associated storage and display mechanisms. A high-level language, in contrast, is designed to mask the internal working of the computer, allowing a programmer to concentrate on the problem and the logic of its solution.

Typically, such a language uses words drawn from human speech to stand for many of its processes, making high-level language programs much easier to read and understand than those written in assembly language. But this vocabulary of so-called keywords or reserved words must be precisely defined — as part of the language — to avoid the possibility of error when programs are translated into instructions for the computer.

The format of the programs themselves must also be very precise. Every language has a set of rules, called its syntax, that dictates the form in which a program can be expressed. The syntax defines the ways that keywords and other elements can be combined to form structures that make up programs. Most high-level languages have many ways to represent data, ranging from simple elements of information to complex data structures. These structures give the programmer the means to organize information so the computer can store and retrieve it efficiently. Similarly, most languages have a diverse selection of control structures, which allow the computer to manipulate the data.

Although syntax varies among different high-level languages and even among different versions of the same language, certain fundamental principles are common to most modern languages. Some of these principles are introduced on the following pages in an imaginary high-level language similar to Pascal, an influential language widely used in teaching programming. The basic data and control structures shown here, though elementary and few in number, can be used to create simple programs, which in turn may be combined to create software such as a computer game or an accounting program.

Declarations and Definitions for Program Clarity

Because a high-level language may be used to create many different kinds of programs, it must be able to represent and work with several types of data. A word-processing program, for instance, manipulates alphanumeric characters, combining them into words and sentences; a financial program handles numerical data and performs mathematical operations. In many applications, in fact, several kinds of data are required. Most modern high-level languages provide methods for distinguishing one kind of data from another and for storing information in a variety of formats.

The most fundamental storage unit is a single element of information, such as a number or a word. Individual units of data storage may also be combined into more complex arrangements, or structures, as shown below. These structures allow the programmer to link related information,

Integer type. Only whole numbers — positive, negative, or zero — can be stored in this data type.

Real type. This type is used to store numbers written with a decimal point (such as 1.5), an exponent (such as 10^{12}) or both.

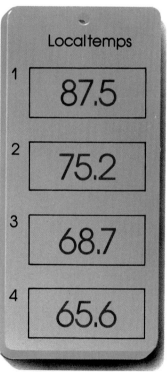

String type. This type can hold one or more characters that may include letters, numbers and other symbols. Often a string is a name or other word.

Boolean type. Named for mathematician and symbolic-logic pioneer George Boole, this type can hold one of two values: true or false.

An array. Several items of the same data type can be grouped in an array. At the beginning of the program the user must declare the identifier, data type and size of each array. An individual element of an array is referred to by a number, called an index, corresponding to its position in the structure. For example, in the array above, identified as *Localtemps*, four real-type elements represent temperature measurements; the value 68.7 is referred to as *Localtemps[3]*.

Data types. Shown as slates of different colors, the four data types of the language illustrated here enable the language to manipulate numbers, words or true-false statements. In this language, the user declares at the beginning of a program the identifiers (shown here as words at the top of each slate) and data types of the variables that will occur in the program. Values (shown below the identifiers) are assigned to variables later.

in the interests of convenience and program efficiency. In a program, an element is given an identifier — a name that helps the programmer keep track of stored information. An identifier refers the computer to a specific memory location where a value is stored; the value is entered separately, by the programmer or by the program itself as it is executed.

A named element may be treated in one of two ways. In preparing the program, the programmer may declare the element to be a constant; once a value is associated with the identifier, it must remain unchanged throughout the execution of the program. Or the element may be declared a variable, whose value may be changed during the program's execution. In a payroll program, for example, if every employee has the same hourly wage, the pay rate would be a constant; variables would include employee names and hours worked.

A language distinguishes among different kinds of information by requiring that constants, variables and elements of more complex data structures be classified by type. Four fundamental types *(below, far left)* allow the programmer to use information in the form of two kinds of numbers, alphanumeric characters, and true-false statements.

In many languages, all data structures and types must be identified in declaration statements at the beginning of each program. This reduces errors and makes the program run more efficiently. The computer may determine in advance how much memory to allot for each piece of information and what kinds of operations may be performed on the different data elements; true-false data elements, for example, generally occupy less space than character strings, and real numbers or integers can be multiplied together while words cannot.

A record. Related elements of different types can be stored in a record. At the beginning of the program, the user gives the record an identifier and declares each element — called a field — by identifier and data type. The record called *Vicepresident*, above, contains three fields: *Name* holds string-type data; *Hired* holds integer-type data; and the field *Married?* holds Boolean-type data, a true-false answer to the question "Is this employee married?" A field is referred to by record and field identifiers: the field *Vicepresident.Name* holds the value *John Brown*.

An array of records. Simple data structures may be combined to form more complex ones, such as an array in which each element is a record. The array treats the records as elements of identical type; each record has the same number of fields, of the same data types but with different values. An item in an array of records is identified by the identifier of the array, the index of the record and the identifier of the field within the record. Thus, in the array called *Employees (above)*, *Employees[2].Hired* identifies the element holding the value 1982.

Special Symbols for Working with Information

The simplest manipulation of data within a program is triggered by operators — words or symbols such as those that tell the computer to multiply two numeric values, to join two string values or to compare the contents of two variables. Operators are combined with data identifiers in constructions called statements — similar to sentences in a human language — that specify tasks for the computer to perform.

Each operator has clearly defined characteristics, working only with specified data types and always producing results

A Sampler of Operators and Functions

Operators. The simple operations shown at right are the result of a program statement called assignment, effected by the operator := (illustrated on the booth on the opposite page), which denotes the assignment of a value to a variable. In the case of the addition at top, the assignment statement was *Sum := FirstNum + SecondNum*. Since the variables *FirstNum* and *SecondNum* are integer-type, the computer interprets the + symbol as an arithmetic operator; it adds the values of the variables and assigns the resulting value, 5, to the variable *Sum*. In the second example, the variables *FirstWord* and *SecondWord* are string-type, so the computer interprets the + symbol as the concatenation operator. It combines the values *cat* and *bird*, assigning *catbird* to *NewWord*.

The third example, of a relational operator, calls for the computer to compare the values held in two integer-type variables. If the value of *Orders* is less than the value of *InStock*, then the value *T* (for true) is assigned to the Boolean-type variable *CanShip*; otherwise, *CanShip* is assigned the value *F* (for false).

FirstNum		SecondNum		Sum
2	+	3	=	5

FirstWord		SecondWord		NewWord
cat	+	bird	=	catbird

Orders		InStock		CanShip
15	≤	78	=	T

Functions. The example at right shows the working of the function *sqrt* for finding a square root. When the value of the integer-type variable *Area* is 2, the computer uses the *sqrt* function to derive the value 1.414, which is assigned to the real-type variable *Side*.

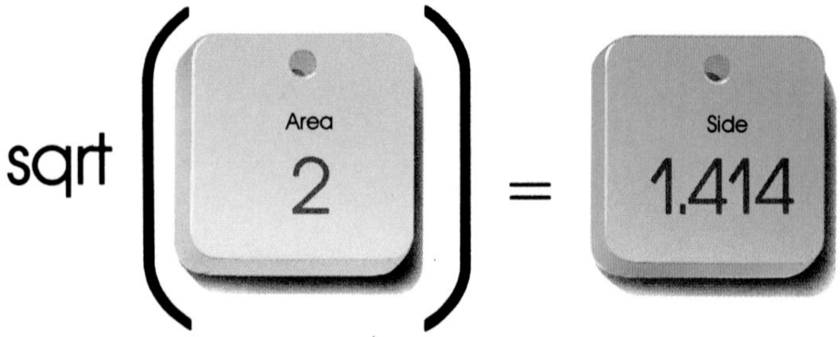

$$\text{sqrt}\left(\,\underset{2}{\text{Area}}\,\right) = \underset{1.414}{\text{Side}}$$

of a given type. In the language shown here, two arithmetic operators — subtraction (-) and multiplication (*) — work only with real or integer types, producing results of the same type. The plus sign (+), in contrast, may be used to add real or integer types as well as to join string-type data in a process called concatenation.

Relational operators make comparisons between two items of the same data type (except Booleans), always producing a true-false result. With numbers, the operators determine whether one is greater than (>), greater than or equal to (≥), equal to (=), less than (<), less than or equal to (≤), or not equal to (<>) the other. With strings, the same operators perform such functions as determining alphabetical order.

More complex manipulations that might be commonly required by programmers are often incorporated into a language as functions (below, left). A function represents the many statements of simple operators that would otherwise be required to perform such tasks as finding a square root.

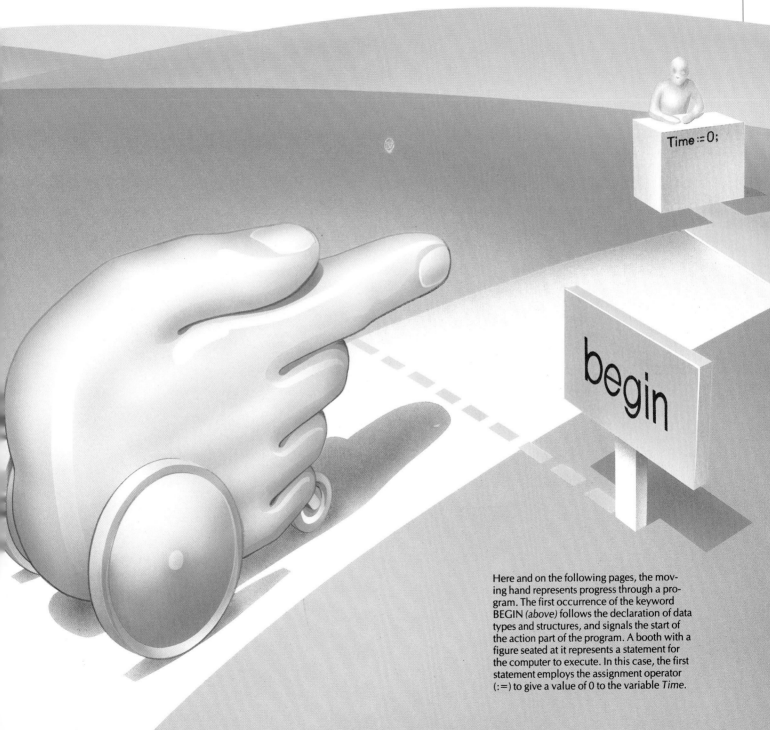

Here and on the following pages, the moving hand represents progress through a program. The first occurrence of the keyword BEGIN (above) follows the declaration of data types and structures, and signals the start of the action part of the program. A booth with a figure seated at it represents a statement for the computer to execute. In this case, the first statement employs the assignment operator (:=) to give a value of 0 to the variable Time.

Moving in Sequence through the Program

As it executes each statement, the computer refers to memory, represented by the billboard below, for the data values required; sometimes a statement changes stored values. In executing $Sum := K + M$, for example, the computer adds the values of K and M, assigning the resulting value to Sum. When the computer executes the next statement, $writeOutput(Sum)$, the new value of Sum will be displayed.

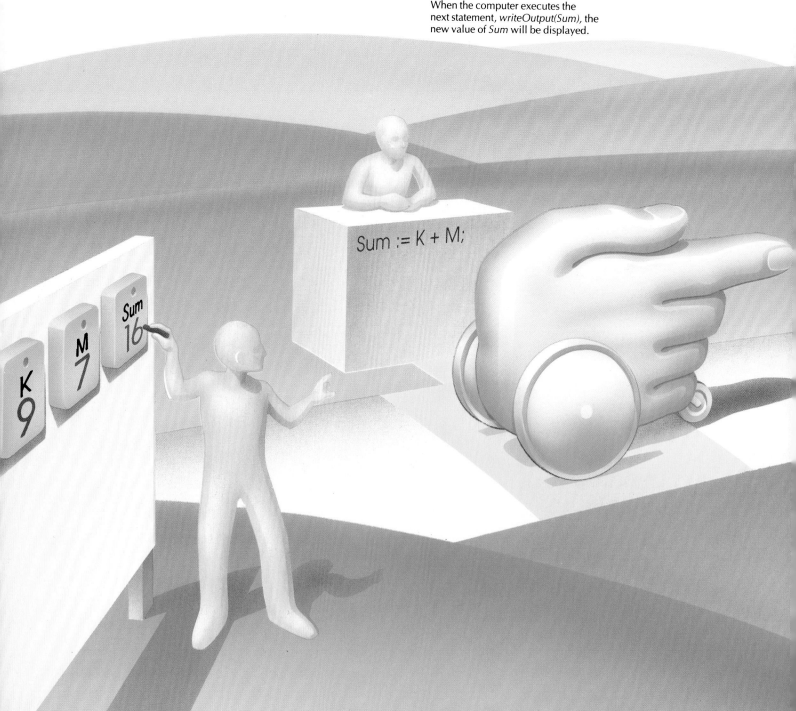

In its most fundamental form, the working part of a program — sometimes called the body — is a series of statements that the computer executes in sequential order: The computer carries out all of the operations specified in one statement before moving on to the next. As in many languages, keywords — here, BEGIN and END — mark the start and finish of the body of the program.

While moving through the program, the computer must refer to the data values stored in its memory. Sometimes these values are changed as a result of the computations specified by a statement. As illustrated below, changing the value does not affect the name or location of a data element; instead, the new value of the element simply replaces the old value. BEGIN and END are only two of the keywords used to regulate the flow of programs. Other keywords help to develop patterns of program execution that are more complex than simple sequential flow; some of these appear in statements on the following pages. Keywords, which are explicitly defined in the language, must be used in strict accordance with the syntax. If a programmer mistakenly used the keyword BEGIN to identify a data element, for example, an error would arise when the program was translated; the word would be treated according to the meaning designated by the language syntax, and the computer would try to begin another program.

The Power of
a Program Branch

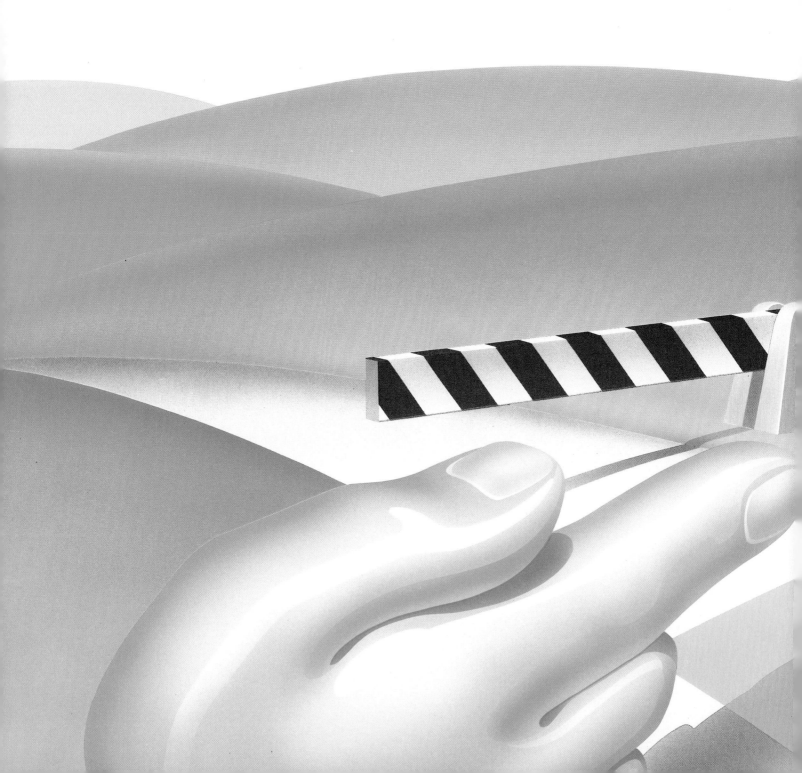

A program may need to be able to choose from among more than one course, performing a different sequence of statements when a specified condition exists in the data being processed. For example, a program that controls an air conditioner might execute one set of statements if the temperature reading is lower than 75° and perform a different sequence when the temperature rises.

This kind of control structure is called a conditional branch; one way it is implemented is by an IF statement, which tells the computer to compare two values and make a choice based on the result of the comparison. Usually the comparison is performed by a relational operator; the IF statement in the air conditioner program might be IF *Temp* ≥ 75 THEN *Cooler* := *on*. Since the relational operator can produce only a Boolean-type result, the IF statement always gets a true or false answer when it compares the value of the *Temp* variable to the number 75. When the condition specified by the keyword IF is true — in this case, when *Temp* is greater than or equal to 75° — the computer performs the action specified after the keyword THEN, assigning the value *on* to the variable *Cooler*. When the condition is false, the computer simply proceeds to the next statement in the program sequence.

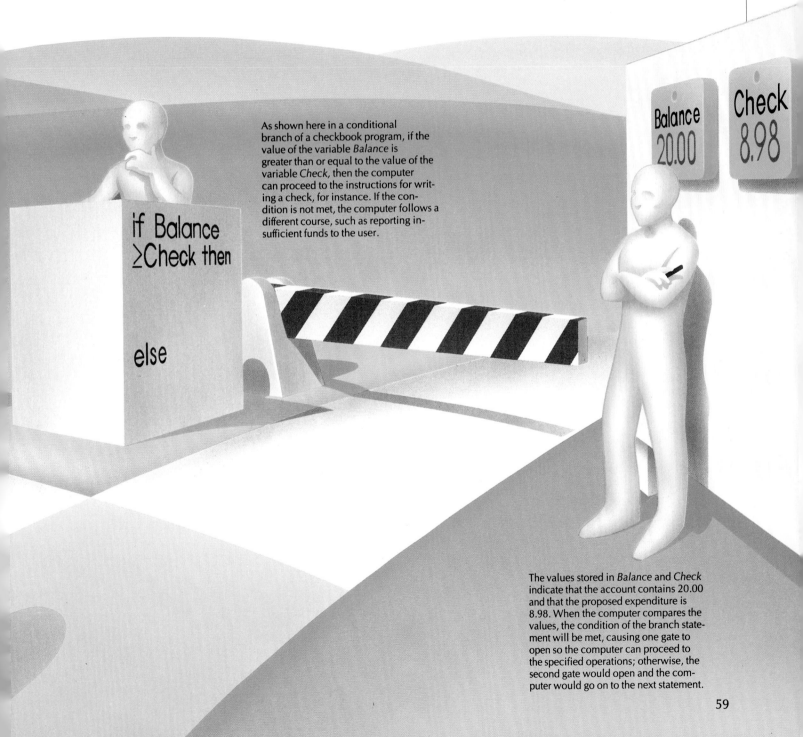

As shown here in a conditional branch of a checkbook program, if the value of the variable *Balance* is greater than or equal to the value of the variable *Check*, then the computer can proceed to the instructions for writing a check, for instance. If the condition is not met, the computer follows a different course, such as reporting insufficient funds to the user.

if Balance
≥Check then

else

Balance
20.00

Check
8.98

The values stored in *Balance* and *Check* indicate that the account contains 20.00 and that the proposed expenditure is 8.98. When the computer compares the values, the condition of the branch statement will be met, causing one gate to open so the computer can proceed to the specified operations; otherwise, the second gate would open and the computer would go on to the next statement.

A Loop to Repeat a Series of Statements

Computers excel at iteration, the performance of repetitive tasks. Most high-level languages allow programmers to exploit this capacity by writing one or more statements in a structure called a loop. One way to begin a loop is with a WHILE statement, which tells the computer to test for a given condition in the data and to repeatedly execute a block of statements as long as that condition exists. When the condition no longer exists, the computer skips over the block to execute the first statement following the loop. A loop may also

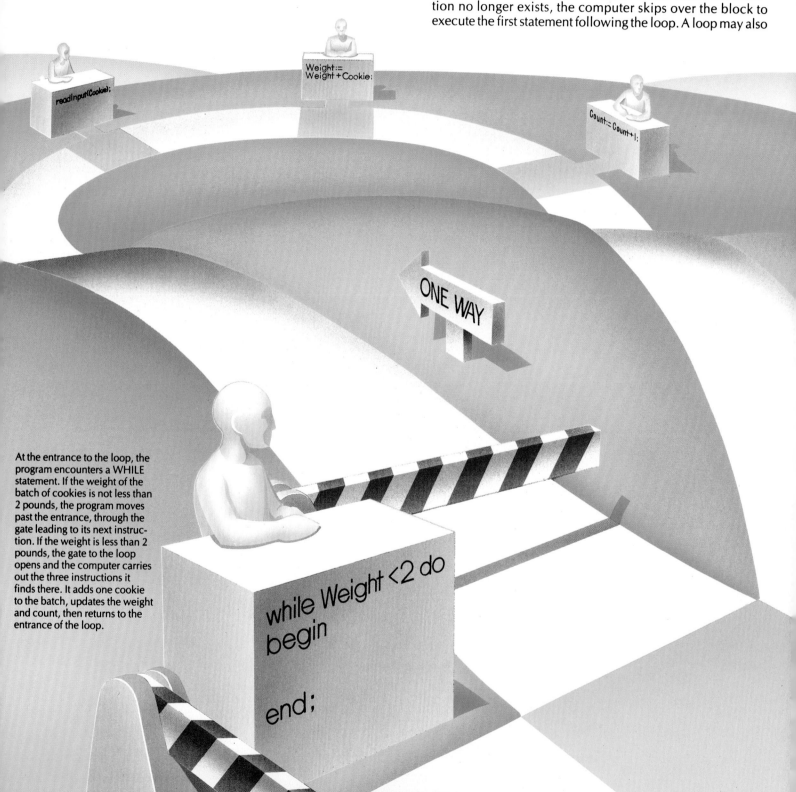

readInput(Cookie);

Weight:=
Weight + Cookie:

Count:= Count+1;

ONE WAY

At the entrance to the loop, the program encounters a WHILE statement. If the weight of the batch of cookies is not less than 2 pounds, the program moves past the entrance, through the gate leading to its next instruction. If the weight is less than 2 pounds, the gate to the loop opens and the computer carries out the three instructions it finds there. It adds one cookie to the batch, updates the weight and count, then returns to the entrance of the loop.

while Weight <2 do
begin

end;

begin with a FOR statement *(pages 62-63)*, which specifies the number of times the computer should execute the loop.

The loop shown here, part of a program to supervise the packing of cookies in 2-pound batches, contains a WHILE statement and three subordinate statements bracketed by the keywords BEGIN and END. The WHILE statement tells the computer to execute the loop as long as the weight of the batch is less than 2 pounds. In the body of the loop, the computer is told first to ascertain the weight of the cookie being added to the batch, then to add that weight to the weight of the batch, and then to add 1 to the running count of cookies in the batch. When the computer encounters the END keyword, it returns to WHILE and checks to see whether the condition that triggers the loop still exists. If it does — in this case, if the batch still weighs less than 2 pounds — the computer starts through the loop again. If the condition no longer exists — when the weight is 2 pounds or more — the computer bypasses the loop and proceeds with the rest of the program.

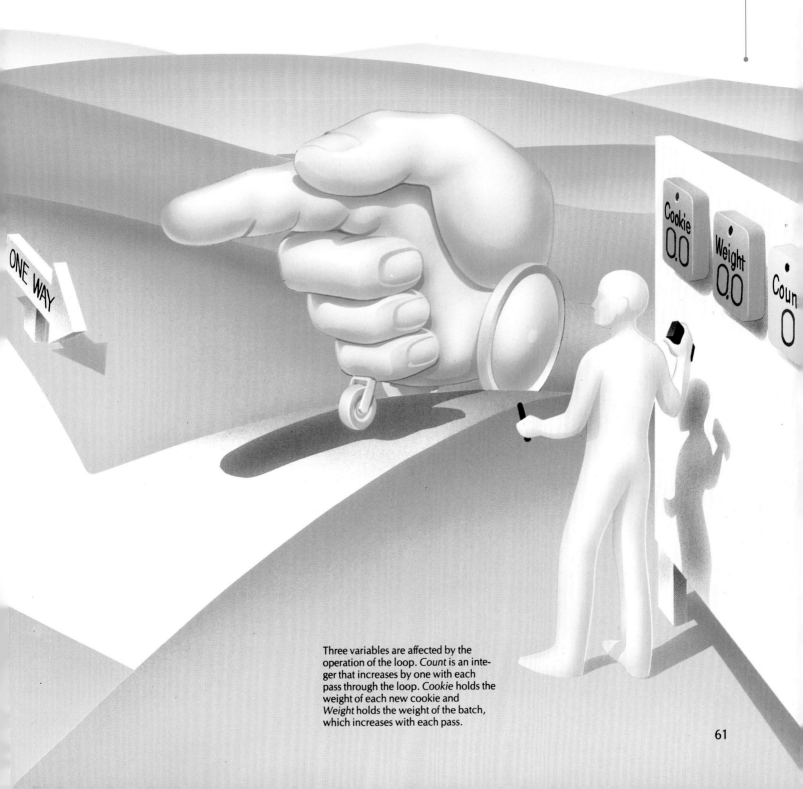

Three variables are affected by the operation of the loop. *Count* is an integer that increases by one with each pass through the loop. *Cookie* holds the weight of each new cookie and *Weight* holds the weight of the batch, which increases with each pass.

Assembling Statements to Build a Program

The numbered statements in the simple program illustrated below correspond to the numbered lines of the listing at right. The program combines several elements of this Pascal-like language to calculate a company's monthly payroll. Data on the board at left can be used, and changed, by any of the program statements.

```
    programPayroll;
1)  type Person = Record
        Name: String;
        Hours,Rate: Real;
        end;
    variables
        Totalpayroll,Salary: Real;
        Numemployed,Count: Integer;
        Month: String;
        Employee: Person;

    begin
2)      readInput(Numemployed);
3)      readInput(Month);
4)      Totalpayroll : = 0.0;
5)      if Numemployed ≥ 1 then
6)          for count : = 1 to Numemployed do

            begin
7)          readInput(Employee.Hours,Employee.Rate,Employee.Nar
8)          Salary : = Employee.Hours * Employee.Rate;
9)          Totalpayroll : = Total payroll + Salary;
10)         writeOutput(Employee.Name,Employee.Hours,Salary);
            end
        else
11)     writeOutput("No employees for this month");
12) writeOutput("For", month, "the payroll is", total payroll);
    end
```

Only a few data and control structures are required to make useful programs. The simple company-payroll program illustrated below combines an IF statement and a loop with a variety of data types to produce a list with each employee's name and pay, as well as the total payroll for the month.

The first line identifies the program name; the next part (**1**) declares its data types and variables. The body of the program commences with BEGIN, followed by *readInput* statements (**2** and **3**), which tell the computer to ask the user for the values of two variables — *Numemployed* (number of employees) and *Month* (the name of the current month). An assignment statement (**4**) sets the initial value of *Totalpayroll* to 0.0 dollars.

An IF-THEN statement (**5**) examines the value of *Numemployed;* if it is less than 1, the company has no employees and the computer proceeds directly to the keyword ELSE (**11**). Otherwise, the program enters a loop that begins with a FOR statement (**6**). This statement tells the computer to repeat the loop delineated by BEGIN and END, adding 1 to the value of the variable *Count* on each pass through the loop; when the value of *Count* equals the value of *Numemployed*, the computer executes the statements of the loop and then returns to sequential flow.

The loop statements tell the computer to get employee data from a record (**7**), calculate that employee's pay for the month (**8**), add that pay to the total payroll (**9**), and append to the payroll list the employee's name, hours and pay (**10**).

The ELSE keyword introduces the final portion (**11**) of the IF-THEN-ELSE statement, which the computer can execute only when the condition stated in the IF statement (**5**) is false. Otherwise, the computer bypasses it, going on to the final statement (**12**), which directs the computer to display the total value of the payroll for the current month.

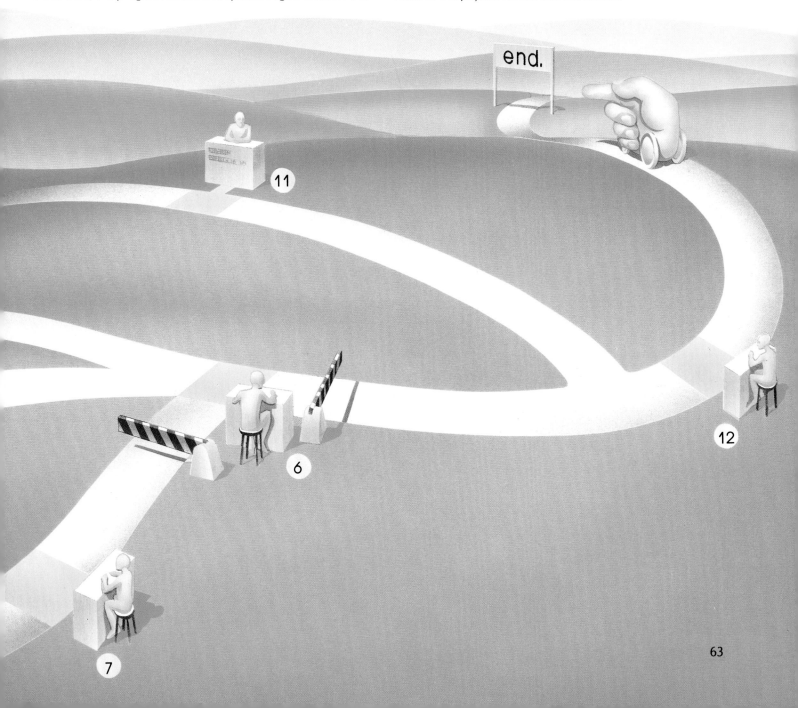

Procedures to Beat Complexity

```
        Procedure Do-one-check (variables Totalpayroll: Real);

1)      variables
            Hours,Rate,Salary: Real;
            Name: String;

        begin
2)          readInput(Hours,Rate,Name);
3)          Salary := Hours * Rate;
4)          Totalpayroll := Totalpayroll + Salary;
5)          writeCheck(Hours,Salary,Name);

        end;
```

As a program becomes more complex, a given job may have to be repeated at different places within the program. Instead of writing the same code each time the job needs to be done, the programmer can save time and effort with a tool called a subroutine, or procedure. Essentially a program within a program, a procedure is a sequence of statements bracketed by the keywords BEGIN and END; this sequence is given a name by which it can be invoked from the main body of the program. Each time the computer encounters the name of a procedure, it transfers control to the procedure and carries out the entire set of statements repre-

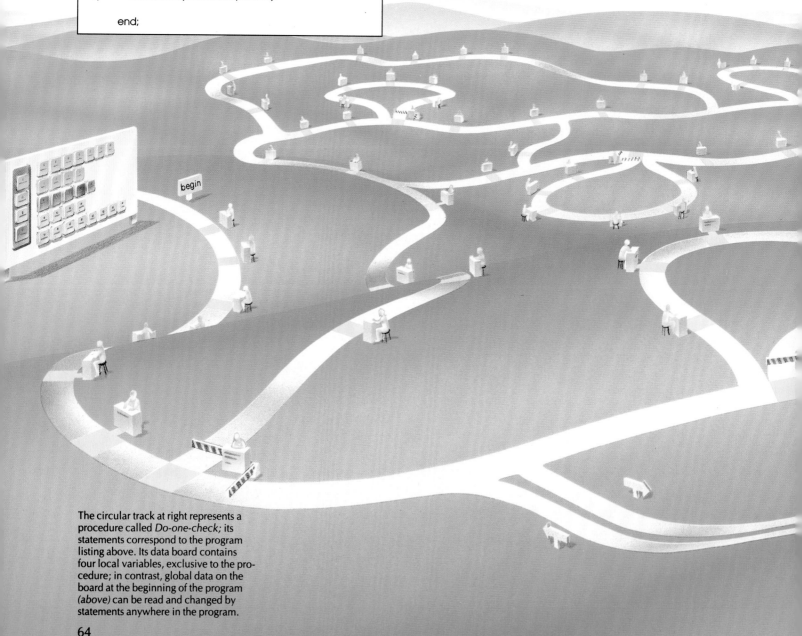

The circular track at right represents a procedure called *Do-one-check;* its statements correspond to the program listing above. Its data board contains four local variables, exclusive to the procedure; in contrast, global data on the board at the beginning of the program *(above)* can be read and changed by statements anywhere in the program.

sented by the name; control then returns to the next step in the main program.

In a payroll program that is more complicated than the one on the preceding pages, the computer might be directed to write a check at several points in the program. As shown in the example below, the check-writing statements can all be incorporated in a procedure called *Do-one-check,* to be used each time a check is required.

The procedure *Do-one-check* contains its own information in the form of local data — data that can be used and changed only by statements within the procedure. Information that needs to be accessible from anywhere in the program is called global data. Establishing these different levels of data prevents some of the errors that might arise in large programs. In such a program, for example, the same variable name might be used by two or more unrelated procedures: If the variable is global, then each time its value is changed by one procedure, the other procedures would also have new, and possibly unexpected, values for the variable. If the variables are local, however, it is impossible for one procedure to interfere with the data of another, even though the same variable names appear in each.

A Dynamic Decade of Development

For a brief time early in the 1960s, the world of computer languages seemed a simple place. Three languages held sway in their large domains: FORTRAN and COBOL pervaded American science and business, and ALGOL 60 was spreading throughout Europe. The newest major language, PL/I, aspired to combine the best features of the other three and be a truly all-purpose tongue.

Beneath the apparent tidiness, however, turbulence reigned. From college and corporate research laboratories, from designers working alone and from the deliberations of prestigious committees, a host of new languages would soon emerge to program the big institutional computers of the day. By the late 1960s, they were proliferating so rapidly that one computer scientist said a language designer "had to know 10 or 12 languages to be socially acceptable."

Some designers occupied themselves with writing entirely new languages, either to fit special needs or because they thought they could devise better ways to communicate with their machines. But programmers also tinkered interminably with compilers for existing languages, making improvements that modified in one way or another the formal rules set forth by a language's original designer.

The result was a bewildering plethora of variations known by such terms as subsets, extensions and dialects. Subsets are versions of a language that incorporate a selection of the features of the full language. Extensions are larger versions that add features to make the language more versatile. And dialects contain minor changes intended to tailor a language to a certain application or to exploit a particular computer's strengths. Dialects are incompatible with their original language and with one another as well; programs written in one dialect cannot be translated into machine code by a compiler written for a different dialect.

This unwieldy state of affairs was amusingly portrayed in 1969 when Jean Sammet published *Programming Languages,* the first comprehensive historical survey of the field. On the book's dust cover and front endpaper was a drawing of a sloppily constructed tower spiraling skyward and displaying the names of precisely 117 different languages. At the top of the tower—the literal point of the illustration—a single word perched as if it were the crowning language of all: BABEL.

Yet this edifice of languages was also a monument to the creativity evident throughout the computer sciences. Programmers did not write new languages merely to exercise their freedom of expression. Computers were reaching rapidly into new and diverse domains, and programmers had to fit languages to the intended use. Today, at least half of all computer languages exist to serve one area of application, such as a branch of engineering or a kind of computer graphics. Unlike FORTRAN and other general-purpose languages—which were originally designed to solve certain kinds of problems but are in fact applicable to

During the 1960s and 1970s, within the imposing institutions of business, academia and the military, vast amounts of money and effort went toward developing new languages to program the machines of the day.

almost any problem — special-purpose languages cannot be used beyond their narrow realm. The oldest of the special-purpose languages still in use is APT, for Automatically Programmed Tools. APT was designed at M.I.T.'s Servomechanisms Laboratory under contract to the U.S. Air Force. Work on the language began in 1957, the same year that FORTRAN, the first popular general-purpose language, was released. The aim was specific: to write programs that, when coded in punched tape and fed into milling machines, would automatically control the cutting and shaping of metal parts for airplanes and other machine-tooled products — in effect, building them by the numbers.

The APT team was headed by Douglas T. Ross, a mathematician and self-taught programmer who was still in his twenties. While pursuing graduate studies at M.I.T., Ross became involved with APT and with other critical air force projects, such as developing a computerized way to evaluate the fire-control system in the B-58 bomber. After months of preliminary work, Ross hammered out the fundamentals of the new language during one marathon weekend in May of 1957, making the notation as much like English as possible in both its semantics and its syntax. The result of his effort was a remarkably simple language for programmers to learn. For example, a program written in APT and designed to cut a specific part employed phrases such as TL DIA/ +1.0, INCH, which meant "the diameter of the cutting tool is one inch."

In 1959, APT and the entire M.I.T.-designed system for computerized control of milling machines were introduced at a press conference at which reporters were given souvenir aluminum ash trays that had been shaped by software written in the new language. Ross noted that one of those present was the legendary broadcaster Lowell Thomas, who could not resist indulging in a pun: With this language, Thomas told his network radio audience, "almost anything was apt to happen."

Much did. The APT system launched today's era of computer-aided manufacturing; now machines automatically produce objects ranging from parts for automobiles and airplanes to artificial limbs for human beings. And computers are highly active in premanufacturing work as well — again, thanks in good measure to Ross's efforts. He oversaw the development of a language called AED (for ALGOL Extended for Design), which was created to write programs for the computer-aided design of parts that then can be turned out by software-controlled machine tools.

A myriad of other special-purpose languages have been used to write software for fields as different as civil engineering, social science research, musical composition, text editing and film making. Some of these languages have spawned new tongues. For example, in the 1960s, two languages known as Movie and Scanner helped to create computerized animation for motion pictures. The pair then produced an offspring called Bug System, or BUGSYS, named not for the feisty cartoon character Bugs Bunny, but for a set of buglike figures that can be moved around on a computer screen. Depending on the command it receives, a bug can change the gray-level value of the picture element, or pixel, on which it is located or mark an area of the screen for visual reference. These features have

This sketch of a computer-age Tower of Babel appeared on the dust jacket of *Programming Languages*, Jean Sammet's overview of the scores of mutually incomprehensible computer languages in use at the time of the book's release in 1969. For a generation of computer scientists, the illustration symbolized the dangerous inefficiency of maintaining a host of languages each of which required its own translating software and trained programmers.

made BUGSYS valuable in scientific research programs, including the analysis of photomicrographs of nerve fibers.

In certain cases, languages initially designed for a particular use are actually extensive enough to qualify as general-purpose. The most notable instances are seen in the field of artificial intelligence, or AI, the branch of computer science that attempts to create programs capable of emulating such human abilities as learning and reasoning.

From the inception of AI in the 1950s, researchers sought a computer language suitable for the manipulation of concepts expressed in human words and phrases. The first attempt was a family of languages called IPL (for Information Processing Languages). It was developed by artificial-intelligence pioneer Allen Newell and his associates, first at the Rand Corporation and then at the Carnegie Institute of Technology (later Carnegie-Mellon) in Pittsburgh, a bastion of AI research. Central to IPL was the idea of the list. By representing data as lists of words and other symbols, a programmer could link concepts in the memory of the computer in a manner roughly analogous to the way AI researchers think ideas are stored in the human brain.

This notion of list processing intrigued another prominent member of the tightly knit AI community, John McCarthy, a brilliant and versatile mathematician. In 1958, the same year he helped establish an AI research lab at M.I.T., McCarthy began work on a high-level language that combined the use of lists with a notation, or set of symbols, borrowed from an esoteric branch of mathematics called the lambda calculus. Introduced in 1931 by mathematician and logician Alonzo Church, the lambda calculus employs only three elements: symbols that represent variables and constants, parentheses for grouping symbols, and a function denotation represented by the Greek letter λ, or lambda. McCarthy called his language LISP, a name derived from shortening the phrase "list processing."

NESTING CODE

Even a small section of a LISP program may include dozens of pairs of list-defining parentheses. Often the parentheses nest within other parentheses, defining lists within lists within lists—sometimes to eight or 10 levels. In the list (PUT(QUOTE SHIP)(QUOTE LOC)(QUOTE (7 5))), for example, the function PUT assigns the Cartesian coordinates (7, 5) to a ship's location; the function QUOTE tells the computer that the user wants to see the name of a list or symbol rather than its value; the symbol LOC is the name of a property—in this case, location—that belongs to the symbol SHIP.

Perhaps the most significant feature of LISP is that data, programs—and even the language itself—are all simply lists of symbols within parentheses. Though difficult to read, this structure makes it possible not only to write programs that can write or modify other programs in turn, but to write programs or subroutines that can refer to themselves in a mathematical process known as recursion *(pages 74-75)*. Both of these aspects of LISP were advantageous in AI's attempts to emulate the complexities of human thought.

Computer scientists admired LISP as much for its elegance as for its utility, especially after McCarthy in 1960 published a widely read paper titled "Recursive Functions in Symbolic Expressions," which detailed LISP's mathematical

In Command of Machines That Tailor Metal

APT, a language created by M.I.T.'s Automatically Programmed Tools project, employs descriptive phrases to command computerized machine tools that produce precisely shaped parts for everything from fighter aircraft to children's toys.

An APT programmer begins by sketching the desired shape of the metal part on a numbered grid, tagging the lines, points and curves with such ordinary English words as BASE and TIP. Then, using this simple anatomical description as a reference, the programmer writes the appropriate instructions, providing three types of information for the computer that will operate the machine tool.

First come specifications regarding the tool, such as the size of its cutting head and the rate at which metal is to be fed past it. Next, the object is described mathematically; the grid's coordinates identify individual points, and the points then serve as reference marks in defining each line and curve. Finally, the programmer lists each motion of the cutting tool as it moves from one named point or curve to another until it is halted by the final instruction: FINI.

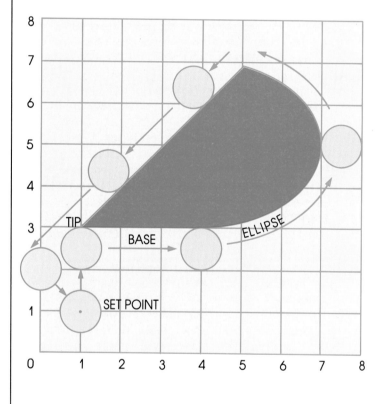

The program in the left-hand column at right contains directions for cutting a simple metal part; the code is explained line-by-line in the right-hand column. Written in the earliest (1959) version of APT, the instructions pilot the cutting tool (represented by the circles on this graph) through a single plane, producing a two-dimensional shape. Fabricating a three-dimensional object would require additional programming.

Part Program	Explanation
CUTTER/1	Use a one-inch-diameter cutter.
TOLER/.005	Tolerance of cut is .005 inch.
FEDRAT/80	Use feed rate of 80 inches per minute.
HEAD/1	Use head No. 1.
MODE/1	Operate tool in mode No. 1.
SPINDL/2400	Turn on spindle. Set at 2,400 rpm.
COOLNT/FLOOD	Turn on coolant. Use flood setting.
PT1 = POINT/4,5	Define a reference point, PT1, as the point with coordinates (4,5).
FROM/(SETPT = POINT/1,1)	Start the tool from the point called SETPT, which is defined as the point with coordinates (1,1).
INDIRP/(TIP = POINT/1,3)	Aim the tool in the direction of the point called TIP, which is defined as the point with coordinates (1,3).
BASE = LINE/TIP, AT ANGL, O	Define the line called BASE as the line through the point TIP that makes an angle of 0 degrees with the horizontal.
GO/TO, BASE	Go to the line BASE.
TL RGT, GO RGT/BASE	With the tool on the right, go right along the line BASE.
GO FWD/(ELLIPS/CENTER, PT1, 3,2,0)	Go forward along the ellipse with center at PT1, semimajor axis = 3, semiminor axis = 2 and major axis making an angle of 0 degrees with the horizontal.
GO LFT/(LINE/2,4,1,3,), PAST, BASE	Go left along the line joining the points (2,4) and (1,3) past the line BASE.
GOTO/SETPT	Go to the point SETPT in a straight line.
COOLNT/OFF	Turn off coolant flow.
SPINDL/OFF	Turn off spindle.
END	This is the end of the machine-control-unit operation
FINI	and the finish of the part program.

underpinnings. "LISP was not merely a language you used to do things," said Paul Abrahams, who had been one of McCarthy's graduate students during the development of the new language. "It was something you looked at: an object of beauty. And ever since, there has been a continual tension between those who love LISP for its purity and those who want to use it to do various kinds of computing. Certainly a lot of computing has been done with LISP. But that wasn't true at the very beginning. It used to be said that the main purpose of LISP was to produce more LISP."

In addition to creating LISP, McCarthy in 1959 proposed the concept of time sharing, which would enable a number of users working at terminals to be served almost simultaneously by one large computer instead of having to wait for their programs to be processed one at a time. His advocacy led to a number of time-sharing projects at M.I.T., and a few years later, two Dartmouth College professors, John Kemeny and Thomas Kurtz, borrowed the idea and implemented it for their introductory courses in computer science. Then, in order to teach the rudiments of programming on their new time-sharing system, Kemeny and Kurtz wrote a simple, easy-to-learn language, modeled on FORTRAN. They called it BASIC (Beginner's All-Purpose Symbolic Instruction Code). BASIC — rich in dialects — was destined to achieve enormous popularity as the grassroots language of the microcomputer revolution that began in the 1970s.

Today, McCarthy's LISP remains the principal programming language for AI research in the United States and ranks as the second-oldest general-purpose language (after FORTRAN) in widespread use. The ease and speed with which programmers can write, run and modify programs in LISP has gained the language adherents beyond the AI laboratory. And, like most popular languages, LISP has its spin-offs. In Great Britain, for example, a common language for AI research is a 1960s derivative of LISP called POP-2, after one of its co-authors at the University of Edinburgh, Robin J. Popplestone.

LISP and all other list-processing languages are classified as procedural. Along with such languages as FORTRAN and COBOL, they give the computer sequences of explicit instructions for arriving at the solution to a problem. By contrast, nonprocedural languages allow the programmer simply to describe the desired result without having to specify exactly how to obtain it. One example of a nonprocedural language is Prolog (for Programming in Logic), designed in 1972 by Alain Colmerauer of the Faculty of Sciences at Luminy in Marseilles.

FACTS, RELATIONSHIPS AND INFERENCES
Rooted in the tradition of formal logic, Prolog has won many enthusiasts in the AI research centers of Europe. The programmer, instead of spelling out step-by-step procedures, can merely provide a set of facts and state the relationships among them (pages 118-121) — that both "truck" and "car," for example, qualify as something called a "vehicle," and that a "vehicle" has something called "wheels." By using these relationships, procedures already built into the language then draw logical inferences — that a "car" has "wheels," for instance. This ability makes Prolog well suited for writing a type of program known as an expert system, the most profitable result thus far of AI research. Expert systems perform feats such as diagnosing a disease or locating a mineral deposit by drawing inferences based on the human expertise embedded in the system.

Virtually all of the list-processing languages, as well as Prolog, emerged from academic settings. Two other important general-purpose languages, however, owe their existence to the research labs of giant corporations. The earlier of these was APL — A Programming Language — which was designed by Kenneth Iverson, a former Harvard professor who had become a staff researcher at IBM. Despite its unassuming name, APL is so different from other languages that a British computer scientist borrowed a line from Oscar Wilde to describe his feelings about it: "I didn't say I liked it, Harry. I said it fascinated me. There is a great difference."

Perhaps APL's most unsettling departure from the norm is its strange appearance. The language is made up of a unique set of 95 characters, consisting of Roman and Greek letters, Arabic numerals and such symbols as diamonds, stars and so-called jots; the main characters are supplemented by about 55 additional symbols created by combining the basic characters. Another difference is this language's extraordinary compactness. APL code can compress into a line or two functions that in other languages might require entire pages or screens full of procedures.

ENIGMATIC NUMBER CRUNCHER

Its unusual character set, combined with its terseness, makes APL so difficult to read that programmers sometimes cannot decipher their own work. However, these characteristics also contribute to one of APL's most appealing features: the power to manipulate large tables of numbers as efficiently as it does a few integers. This ability in effect restores the computer to its original role as a high-powered calculator capable of rapidly processing reams of statistics and other numerical data.

The origins of APL date to the late 1950s, when Iverson, a self-described "renegade from mathematics," was teaching computing courses at Harvard. His intention in developing APL was not to create a programming language but to devise a notation for clearly and concisely expressing mathematical ideas about computing for his classroom lectures and for a book he co-authored, *Automatic Data Processing.*

Iverson later explained that his ideas about programming were greatly influenced by another renegade from mathematics, his Harvard mentor Howard Aiken, who had been the motivating genius behind Harvard's first computer, the Mark I. "Although he had a very theoretical turn of mind," Iverson said of Aiken, "he always spoke of himself as an engineer. And he characterized an engineer as being a man who could build for one buck what any damn fool could build for ten. He also emphasized simplicity, and one of the most striking things that I think all of his graduate students remember was, when faced with the usual sort of enthusiastic presentation of something, he would say, 'I'm a simple man. I don't understand that. Could you try to make it clear?' "

Iverson's APL reflected Aiken's demand for clarity, but it remained no more than a notation on paper for several years. Then in 1960, after being denied tenure at Harvard, Iverson joined IBM's staff at the Thomas J. Watson Research Center in Yorktown Heights, New York. There, in collaboration with engineer Adin Falkoff and others, he designed APL's unconventional character

set and later directed the team that implemented the language on the IBM System/360 computer. Company officials provided little encouragement; they were preoccupied at the time with what was known as the "one-language policy"—promoting PL/I as the all-purpose language. The corporation's benign neglect actually proved beneficial. It enabled Iverson and Falkoff to experiment with APL and refine it without pressure from top management or from IBM customers. In 1966, IBM programmers who began using the new language on an experimental time-sharing system found they liked APL's ability to solve complex problems quickly and easily. When word of this new tool got out, potential users started petitioning IBM for the release of APL to the public.

In 1969, more than 500 people attended an APL conference at IBM's headquarters in Armonk, New York. The meeting stirred up such a storm of demands for APL's distribution that participants later referred to the event as "The March on Armonk." A few months later, IBM reluctantly released the language, but without the fanfare — or the technical support — that the company is capable of generating. APL nevertheless quickly gained a devoted following among business analysts and others: It was the first language to have a special-interest group — or SIG, as such groups are known — sponsored by the Association for Computing Machinery (ACM), an international scientific and educational society for computer professionals.

Within a few years of APL's unostentatious debut, another language emerged from a corporate lab. C was developed at the American Telephone & Telegraph Company's Bell Laboratories in Murray Hill, New Jersey, where a participant characterized the atmosphere as one of "salutary neglect." No company official had ordered a new language, nor was there any particular market for one. C resulted instead from friendly competition among a small group of Bell programmers seeking a language to use as they experimented with new software. "There were no projects, no specs, no requirements," recalled a member of the group. "It was almost all done on speculation."

AN ALPHABETIC CHRISTENING

Indeed, the name C came into being almost as casually as the language itself. C was simply the name given the successor to an earlier in-house language called B. (B, for its part, was derived from a language developed at Cambridge University known as BCPL — Basic Combined Programming Language — which itself was a descendant of ALGOL 60.)

C was designed in 1972 by Dennis Ritchie, a 31-year-old systems programmer who had joined Bell four years earlier after earning a Ph.D in applied mathematics at Harvard. Ritchie hoped his new language could be employed to program another unofficial project that was coming to fruition at Bell Labs: a new computer operating system called UNIX, designed by Ken Thompson, considered by some of his peers to be the best programmer in the world. An operating system is a collection of programs that perform such fundamental tasks as taking in, storing and putting out information, and providing an interface between the computer's circuitry and its applications programs. Traditionally, operating systems are written in low-level assembly language for greater speed, but C proved so successful in this role that it eventually was used to write more

Many of the 150 or so characters of the APL language are unique to that tongue. Although APL programmers use conventional letters and numbers as well, they are able to abbreviate their work considerably by calling up specific mathematical functions with single keystrokes. The character above, for example, instructs a computer to find the integer closest to but less than the value of each number in a list of numbers — a job that can require a page of code in a less powerful language.

Repetition through Recursion

The program name is MIRROR IMAGE;

Before starting the action part of the program, note the definition of procedure Do-One-More.

1) Reserve a new space in memory big enough to hold one character.
2) Read one character from a file.
3) If the character is not a period, then "Do-One-More" (make a new copy of the procedure and execute it).
4) Display the character on the screen.

BEGIN action part of the program MIRROR IMAGE

    Do-One-More;

END of program.

The program MIRROR IMAGE consists of one instruction — a call to the four-step recursive procedure named *Do-One-More*. The procedure holds a space in memory and sends the first character it receives to that space. Since the character was not a period, the program moves on to the instruction *Do-One-More*, copies the procedure and begins again.

1) Reserve a new space in memory big enough to hold one character.
2) Read one character from a file.
3) If the character is not a period, then "Do-One-More" (make a new copy of the procedure and execute it).

1) Reserve a new space in memory big enough to hold one character.
2) Read one character from a file.
3) If the character is not a period, then "Do-One-More" (make a new copy of the procedure and execute it).

1) Reserve a new space in memory big enough to hold one character.
2) Read one character from a file.
3) If the character is not a period, then "Do-One-More" (make a new copy of the procedure and execute it).

1) Reserve a new space in memory big enough to hold one character.
2) Read one character from a file.
3) If the character is not a period, then "Do-One-More" (make a new copy of the procedure and execute it).

1) Reserve a new space in memory big enough to hold one character.
2) Read one character from a file.
3) If the character is not a period, then "Do-One-More" (make a new copy of the procedure and execute it).
4) Display the character on the screen.

4) Display the character on the screen.

4) Display the character on the screen.

4) Display the character on the screen.

4) Display the character on the screen.

The program name is REVERSE;

Before starting the action part of the program, reserve enough space in memory to hold the following:

A) 100 characters of input
B) An integer (whole number) for counting

BEGIN action part of the program REVERSE

1) Set the initial value of counter to 1.
2) While no period has been read and while there are no more than 100 characters, repeat the following steps:
2A) Read one character from a file.
2B) Store it in the next available memory location as indicated by the counter.
2C) Increase the counter by 1.
3) Once either a period has been read or the counter has exceeded 100, display all the characters stored in step 2B in reverse order, starting with the highest value of the counter and counting down to 1.

END of program.

To perform the same MIRROR IMAGE task with iteration, the program must supply more detailed instructions, reserving the maximum amount of memory, and telling the machine how to store and retrieve each character.

Recursion, like iteration *(pages 60-61)*, is a programming technique that causes an operation or set of operations to be repeated. But iteration requires the programmer to specify, among other things, how many times to repeat a step and how much space to reserve in memory for the results of each operation — a level of detail that can be inefficient if not impossible to provide. In looking for relationships in the large, varying data bases characteristic of artificial-intelligence programs, for example, the programmer often cannot declare all conditions in advance.

Recursion lets the programmer focus on finding the solution to the problem rather than on the mechanics of imple-menting the solution. In one type of recursion — illustrated here by MIRROR IMAGE, a program to display letters in reverse order — a program can invoke itself as a procedure, or subprogram. At some point, the program pauses to create, in effect, a copy of itself, then executes the copy, which in turn stops to make another copy, and so on. When a predetermined circumstance occurs, the cycle halts; the last copy is executed all the way through, and the remaining steps in each next-higher level are executed until the original program is finished. Detailed instructions are spelled out only once, and memory is requisitioned only as needed, allowing the program to tackle problems of varying sizes.

Each time the procedure *Do-One-More* calls itself, a new copy of the procedure is made. Each succeeding copy reserves a space in memory and stores the next character using a method of storage called "last in, first out," or LIFO. The character stored by the first copy of the procedure is on the bottom of the stack, the last character at the top.

When the active copy of the procedure *(red)* receives a period, it carries out its fourth instruction, sending the period from memory to the screen. The preceding copy *(pink)* then executes its fourth instruction, and so on until control of the program has returned to the original set of instructions, and .STAR — mirror image of RATS. — appears on the screen.

than 90 percent of all the code in the kernel program of the UNIX system.

Prohibited by antitrust regulations from selling UNIX, AT&T effectively gave away the system to colleges and other nonprofit institutions, charging only a small licensing fee. As UNIX gained adherents, C became popular as a so-called medium-level language, combining the convenience, brevity and portability of a high-level language with the direct and efficient access to hardware characteristic of an assembly language. Programmers working with various aspects of computer graphics have found C useful for such tasks as generating special effects for the movie *Return of the Jedi* and enhancing the images that gave seagoing scientists their first look at the wreck of the *Titanic*.

FUROR AND CONTROVERSY

The unpressured atmosphere that enabled APL and C to flourish was not typical of most language development. More often, the birth of a new language was attended by furious debate. In Europe, the ferment of the 1960s swirled around controversial attempts to improve upon the highly regarded programming language ALGOL 60. As early as 1962, a new ALGOL committee was formed by the International Federation for Information Processing (IFIP). Its mission was, first, to design a subset that would eliminate some of the less workable features of ALGOL 60, and then to create an enhanced successor language.

The assignment was straightforward enough, but it led to a long season of turmoil and dissension. An insider's view of what happened in the ALGOL committee over the next six years eventually was provided by a British member, C.A.R. Hoare, of Oxford University. The occasion for these revelations was Hoare's lecture as the 1980 recipient of the Turing Award, the highest honor for technical contribution conferred by the Association for Computing Machinery.

When Hoare began his work with the ALGOL committee, he was a promising young programmer for a small computer manufacturer. "I greatly welcomed the chance of meeting and hearing the wisdom of many of the original language designers," he recalled. "I was astonished and dismayed at the heat and even rancor of their discussions. Apparently the original design of ALGOL 60 had not proceeded in that spirit of dispassionate search for truth which the quality of the language had led me to suppose." The committee at length agreed on the requested subset; the real problems began when members tackled the question of a successor language. In 1965, Hoare and a Swiss member, Niklaus Wirth, who was then teaching at Stanford University, submitted a modest revised version that Hoare felt "consolidated the best features of ALGOL 60 while eliminating its trouble spots." This version, which came to be known as ALGOL W in honor of Wirth, was eventually published and found many users on university campuses, but the committee rejected it.

There followed a succession of other proposals. As Hoare put it, each of these was "a longer and thicker document, full of errors corrected at the last minute, describing equally obscurely yet another different, and to me, equally unattractive language." Few members paid heed to Hoare's criticisms of the evolving design's "obscurity, complexity and overambition." In fact, Hoare said, members took advantage of repeated delays in the committee's work to pack the would-be successor language with even more complex features, instead of trying to simplify it.

In 1968, after five years as a visiting professor at Stanford University, Swiss computer scientist Niklaus Wirth *(shown here at home near Zurich)* returned to Switzerland to begin work on Pascal. The language would soon become the standard tool for teaching computer programming.

"At last, in December 1968," Hoare went on, "in a mood of black depression, I attended the meeting in Munich at which our long-gestated monster was to come to birth and receive the name ALGOL 68." Hoare, Wirth and other prominent dissidents protested the approval of the new language. They even filed a minority report — later suppressed by the IFIP parent body — stating that "as a tool for the reliable creation of sophisticated programs, the language was a failure." As the dissidents predicted, ALGOL 68 proved too cumbersome to win the rapid acceptance in Europe that had greeted its predecessor, ALGOL 60. Accomplished programmers had difficulty understanding even the document that defined the new language. For years, only one institution, the Royal Signals and Radar Establishment, had an actual ALGOL 68 compiler in use.

Out of the debacle, however, arose an elegant new language, one that would influence programmers everywhere for years to come. Its name was Pascal, after the 17th-century French mathematician-philosopher Blaise Pascal, and its author was Niklaus Wirth. Wirth began writing Pascal in 1968, the same year that he and Hoare failed in their efforts to prevent the approval of ALGOL 68. By then, he was a professor of computer science at the Swiss Federal Technical University (site of the original ALGOL 58 meeting), and he wanted a tool for teaching his students sound programming practices. Wirth was dissatisfied, he said, not only with the new ALGOL but also with all of "the presently used major languages whose features and constructs too often cannot be explained logically and convincingly and which too often represent an insult to minds trained in systematic reasoning."

AN ENGINEER'S APPROACH

Wirth, whose teen-age passion for building and flying radio-controlled model airplanes had led to a doctorate in electrical engineering from the University of California in 1963, tackled the problem of designing a language as an engineer might approach the building of a machine. "If one views programming as the design of a machine," Wirth wrote, "the need for precision becomes all the more obvious." The art in engineering, he said on another occasion, "is to make a complicated problem simpler."

Wirth's new language reflected this outlook. In a separate section at the beginning of a program, a Pascal programmer must define all the variables and state explicitly each data type — whether the contents of a given variable will be treated as integers for computation, for example, or as a string of characters. Pascal also encourages a logical structure that divides a program into many simple tasks.

By enforcing such discipline, Pascal limits the programmer's freedom. But the language also fosters a rigorous programming style that makes it far more difficult to commit errors. And Pascal's structure renders programs much more readable, enabling people other than the original programmer to find and correct whatever bugs there might be and to make other changes.

As a result, Pascal is especially well suited for teaching the theory and techniques of programming, but not for writing practical applications. For example, Pascal, like ALGOL, made no provisions for input and output in the formal language itself. From Wirth's point of view, machine-specific considerations such as reading data from the keyboard or writing data to external storage were irrelevant to learning the logic of programming; compilers written for real-life computers would each handle those facilities differently.

Pascal's success vastly exceeded Wirth's modest expectations. Colleges on both sides of the Atlantic adopted it as the classroom tool for teaching programming to aspiring computer scientists. Perhaps most important, Pascal became the bellwether of a movement just beginning to build steam in the early 1970s. The so-called structured-programming movement, aimed at reforming the way computer software is put together, gained impetus from *Structured Programming,* a seminal book published in 1972 by Britain's C.A.R. Hoare, O. J. Dahl of Norway and the iconoclastic Dutch computer scientist, Edsger Dijkstra.

AN EMPHASIS ON LOGIC
Though the phrase has come to mean practically all things to all programmers, essentially it describes a systematic, mathematical approach to the creation of software. In particular, it calls for dividing programs into small, logically arranged tasks, as Pascal does. One specific aim of structured programming is to reduce the use of the so-called unconditional jump, or GOTO statement. Most major languages use the GOTO in order to transfer control of processing from one place in a program to another point perhaps several pages distant. Though a handy tool for the programmer, the GOTO statement almost always makes a program more difficult to read and thus increases the chance that errors will go undetected.

By stressing rigorous organization, advocates of structured programming hoped to limit the problems created by the ever-increasing complexity of software. Programs such as those required by systems that control air traffic — and later space satellites — were growing so large that they took years to complete; they had to be written in sections by teams of programmers, none of whom had a grasp of how everything fit together. Too often the result was software that cost millions of dollars, lagged months behind schedule and came on-line containing thousands of errors. The problem became so severe that computer scientists started referring to it as "the software crisis."

Nowhere was this mounting crisis more critical than in the U.S. military establishment, the world's largest consumer of computer hardware and software. By 1973, when officials began to pay serious attention to the problem, the Department of Defense was spending nearly half of its $7.5 billion computer budget to develop and maintain software. The cost of computer hardware, by contrast, was declining despite dramatic improvements in the computers' power and memory.

The software problem was most acute in weaponry and other so-called embedded computer systems. Such a system consists of a computer embedded in a weapon or machine — the tiny computer in a ballistic missile, for example, or the bigger ones controlling the communications on an airplane or ship. (Examples of embedded systems in nonmilitary applications include the microprocessors in automobiles or microwave ovens as well as the ones in robots on an industrial assembly line.)

Programs for embedded military systems often run to tens of thousands of lines of code. Expensive to write, such programs are even more costly to maintain. Over a typical lifetime of up to 20 years, they must undergo repeated modifications to keep up with the system's changing requirements. And program bugs in a system controlling a ballistic missile or an air-defense network could obviously have disastrous consequences.

No small part of the problem was the incredible hodgepodge of languages in which embedded-system software was written. Surveys during the early 1970s found no fewer than 450 high-level languages and dialects employed in coding such programs. (Some estimates, which also counted assembly languages, ran as high as 1,500.) Many were obscure languages developed for a single job because none of the major general-purpose languages could meet the job's special needs. These needs might include unusual input/output requirements and real-time control — the ability to monitor and respond to constantly changing conditions.

One result of the proliferation of languages in the military was massive duplication of effort. Each service had its own favorite languages, which were incompatible with those of the other services; a program written in an air force language, for example, had to be completely rewritten in a different language for use by the army or the navy. This, together with the related problems of training programmers to make them literate in more than one language, and of developing separate compilers for many applications, added up to runaway costs.

In January 1975, the Pentagon set out to impose order on the linguistic chaos. It established a large committee known as the High Order Language Working Group (HOLWG), with representatives from all the military services as well as from three U.S. allies in the North Atlantic Treaty Organization — France, West Germany and the United Kingdom. HOLWG's mandate was to find languages — preferably only a few of them — suitable for programming every new embedded computer system that came on-line.

THE AIR FORCE'S COMPUTER JOCKEY

HOLWG's chairman, and the driving force behind the effort to straighten out the software mess, was Air Force Lieutenant Colonel William Whitaker. A brilliant student who dreamed of becoming a jet pilot, Whitaker had breezed through his undergraduate studies in physics at Tulane University in two years. He then achieved the highest academic grades in the history of his air force flight school — only to wash out as a pilot because he just could not get the hang of controlling an airplane. Despite this disappointment, Whitaker stayed in the air force and became thoroughly versed in computer science during a 16-year stint in nuclear weapons research at Kirtland Air Force Base, near Los Alamos, New Mexico. While rising to the post of chief scientist of the Air Force Weapons Laboratory there, he personally accounted for some 30,000 hours of computer processing time.

During that period, Whitaker came to know the frustrations of language incompatibility all too well. He remembered one program in particular that had to be rewritten five times as his computers again and again were replaced by newer models. Though HOLWG's mandate did not require the creation of a single common language, Whitaker had that in mind from the beginning. "He believed, when no one else believed, that there was a need for a common language," recalled one close observer, "and then he made it happen."

The way Whitaker made it happen was a sharp departure from all of the language-design procedures that had gone before, either in or out of the military. Instead of appointing a committee to haggle endlessly and then settle upon a language, HOLWG — at Whitaker's urging — sought the guidance of a long list of computer users within the military and programming experts outside.

The users were asked to help define the necessary requirements for a common language. The task of drafting these general specifications fell to David Fisher, a civilian researcher at the Institute for Defense Analyses. Fisher brought to the job a solid background in the theory and practice of programming; he had taught at two universities and had designed military software at the Burroughs Corporation. He already had conducted studies of the Defense Department's software costs and understood its tangle of computer languages so thoroughly that he could usually pinpoint in an instant which department installation used which dialect of which language, and what the dialect's particular features were meant to achieve.

A STRAWMAN'S FATE
In April 1975, three months after the formation of HOLWG, Fisher's first draft of requirements for a common language was circulated to reviewers in the military, industry and academia under the code name Strawman. The choice of name was significant, indicating that Fisher and Whitaker intended this document, as someone put it, "to have the stuffing knocked out of it" by the reviewers, who would then suggest improvements.

The pounding was not long in coming, and Strawman was revised in response to the critical comments. This cycle of draft, review and revision continued

Milestones of Language Development

In a field where innovations are frequently obsolescent by the time they enter the marketplace, computer languages have been remarkably stable. The majority of the most influential programming languages were released between 1955 and 1960 and, with a few notable exceptions — such as the nonprocedural AI language called Prolog — those that came after were variations on well-established themes. For example, JOVIAL, released in 1960, is the United States Air Force's version of ALGOL 58.

On the time line that begins at right and continues on the following pages, dates generally refer to the years in which the languages were released to the public. Dates for pioneers such as Plankalkül and EDSAC assembly language, which were never available commercially, reflect the year in which the language's designer completed work on it.

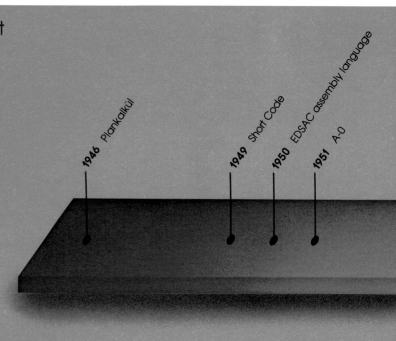

1946 Plankalkül

1949 Short Code

1950 EDSAC assembly language

1951 A-0

through five additional sets of requirements over the following three years, eventually reflecting evaluations by more than 80 review teams in the U.S. and Europe. Each succeeding document bore a name that measured progress toward a hardening of the requirements: Woodenman, Tinman, Ironman, Revised Ironman and, the final standard, Steelman.

The list of requirements lengthened, reaching nearly 100 by the Tinman phase, until it became clear that no existing language could fill them all. The armed services issued an interim list of seven languages, including FORTRAN and COBOL, approved for programming embedded systems. But subsequent appraisals of these and a score of others made clear that none could satisfy more than 75 percent of the specified requirements.

Under Whitaker's prodding — "he ran the project with an iron fist," an observer noted, "in a velvet glove, of course" — HOLWG came to agree that the requirements could be met only by creating an entirely new language. To achieve this, the committee decided to stage an unprecedented international competition. In May 1977, while the specifications were still evolving, the committee requested proposals from the world's top language designers, with the understanding that the proposals would be based on one of three languages: PL/I, ALGOL 68 or Pascal. Fifteen design teams responded, and most of their proposals were based on Pascal, demonstrating the dramatic impact of the new concept of structured programming.

HOLWG selected four of the proposals for funding during a six-month preliminary design phase. The contractors, all of whom proposed Pascal-based designs, were two Massachusetts companies, SofTech and Intermetrics; a Cali-

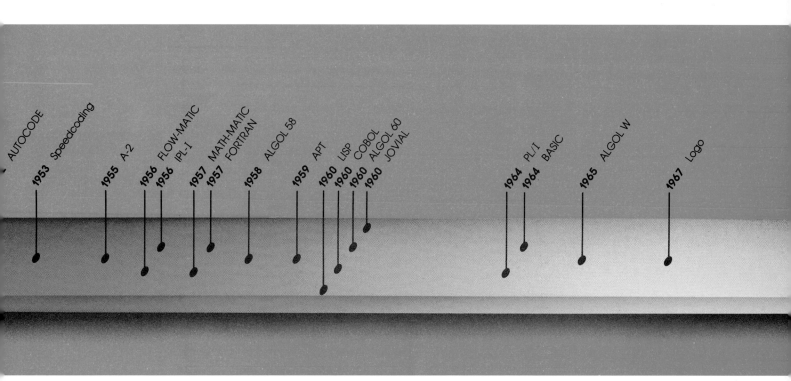

AUTOCODE   1953 Speedcoding   1955 A-2   1956 FLOW-MATIC   1956 IPL-I   1957 MATH-MATIC   1957 FORTRAN   1958 ALGOL 58   1959 APT   1960 LISP   1960 COBOL   1960 ALGOL 60   1960 JOVIAL   1964 PL/I   1964 BASIC   1965 ALGOL W   1967 Logo

fornia firm, SRI International; and Cii Honeywell Bull, the Paris-based subsidiary of an American company, Honeywell Corporation. Though each design team's entry received a color code name to preserve its anonymity during the review process, the predilections of the contractors were so familiar that astute reviewers were able to match the teams with their respective designs in a matter of minutes.

In 1978, after evaluation by nearly 400 reviewers, two of the four designs—Red (Intermetrics) and Green (Cii Honeywell Bull)—were selected for a final showdown. The year-long phase of refinement that followed was unusually intense. A member of the Red team remembered falling asleep at night crying from fatigue. "Red was the more conservative language, Green the more briefly described, avant-garde language," one of the competitors said. "But both languages changed during this final phase: Red becoming more avant-garde, Green becoming more conservative as it was fleshed out."

The winner, announced in May of 1979, was Cii Honeywell Bull. The Green team's victorious entry was christened Ada. The name honored Augusta Ada, Countess of Lovelace, the 19th-century mathematician and writer who is often credited with being the world's first programmer because of her interpretive writings about Charles Babbage's Analytical Engine in the predawn history of computing.

The victory was a personal triumph for Jean Ichbiah, who headed the Green team. Born in Paris in 1940, Ichbiah trained as a civil engineer at the prestigious École Polytechnique. Later, the French government awarded him a fellowship for further study in the United States. He became so captivated by computer pro-

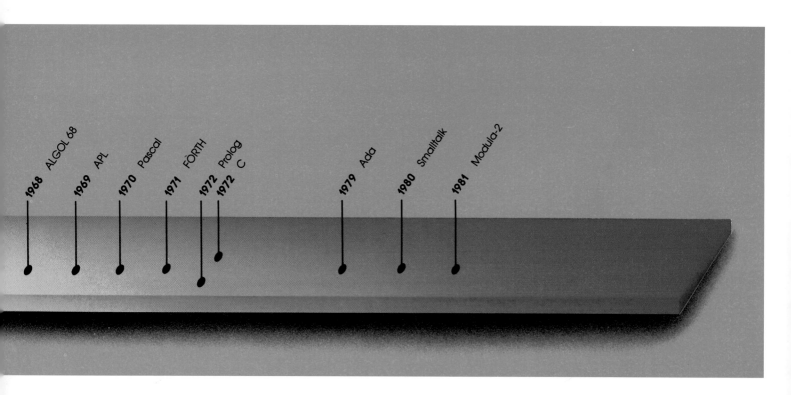

gramming while taking his Ph.D. at M.I.T. that he had difficulty completing his thesis on the optimal arrangement of subway systems. Soon thereafter, Ichbiah joined Cii, a new French company that later merged into Cii Honeywell Bull, and in 1972 he designed his first programming language, LIS, for *Langage d'Implementation de Systèmes*. LIS was strongly influenced by Pascal and was the seed from which Ada sprang.

During the design competition, Ichbiah, who spoke no fewer than five human languages and had a brown belt in judo, drove himself even harder than he drove his 10-person international team, which included members from the U.S., the United Kingdom and West Germany as well as France. He sometimes worked 100 hours a week perfecting the design. Often he let his intuition guide him in making a decision, relying on esthetic considerations, for example, before developing a logical rationale. The result, wrote an admiring member of the runner-up Red team, was not "a language designed by a committee" but one "designed by a small team with a strong leader."

MODULES FOR EASY MAINTENANCE

Ada's most distinctive aspect was an extreme approach to structured programming. The language permitted programs to be written in packages — self-contained modules that can be produced by different programmers and then fitted together. A package can be designed, tested, debugged and then stored in a library for later use in a program as if it were a piece of off-the-shelf software. This modular scheme, Ada's advocates have argued, creates programs that are reliable, easy to read and easy to maintain, saving thousands of hours and hundreds of millions of dollars.

But Ada's fans concede that the language pays a price for its readability and other advantages. Ada has so many features, designed to meet the government's Steelman specifications, that it is exceedingly difficult to learn. In addition, an Ada compiler occupies many more times the memory space needed by compilers for its root language, Pascal. Ada's size and complexity bothered critics such as Pascal's author, Niklaus Wirth, and C.A.R. Hoare, his old colleague from the ALGOL 68 controversy. Hoare, who served with Wirth on the SRI International team that was eliminated in the semifinals of the design competition, worried aloud that "gadgets and glitter prevail over fundamental concerns of safety and economy." He even publicly raised the specter of missiles going awry because of an undetected flaw in an Ada compiler.

Wirth put his concern a different way. "It throws too many things at the programmer," he said. "I don't think you can just learn a third of Ada and be fine. There are places where you tread on one of these spots which you haven't learned about, and it backfires on you."

In defense of his language, Ada's chief architect, Jean Ichbiah, expressed his "admiration and respect" for Wirth but added: "There are times when Wirth believes in small solutions for big problems. I don't believe in that sort of miracle. Big problems need big solutions!"

Other advocates have contended that the only alternative to a large, complex language like Ada for writing big software projects is a proliferation of small, simple and incompatible languages — the very situation that Ada was meant to remedy.

Predictably, creating compilers that would allow Ada programs to run efficiently on the Defense Department's various machines was no easy task. The job was made even more difficult by the Pentagon's determination that Ada remain unadulterated by dialects, extensions or subsets. Under the department's Ada copyright, any proposed compiler must conform to uncommonly rigid standards: No one can call their product an Ada compiler unless it is first officially validated in a battery of some 2,000 tests.

THE SURVIVORS AT WORK

Despite these hurdles, successful compilers eventually appeared, and Ada began to make its presence felt. In 1983, the Defense Department directed that all new "mission-critical" applications be written in Ada. "Mission-critical" refers to computerized communications and weapons systems, such as the enormous programs contemplated for the Strategic Defense Initiative antimissile network. By the end of the decade; 85 percent of new mission-critical software—an estimated five billion dollars' worth—had been written in Ada.

Beyond its military applications, which included adoption as NATO's standard programming language, Ada has made modest headway. One lifesaving program that takes advantage of Ada's real-time capabilities monitors the condition of hospital patients connected to kidney dialysis machines. And although critics of the language remain vocal, Ada's absolute uniformity makes it irresistible to many managers of large programs.

Other major languages have gone through the tedious process of standardization, under the auspices of the American National Standards Institute (ANSI), in an attempt to rein in their dialects. But no other recent language has been so vigorously standardized from the outset, before dialects could even begin to proliferate. Thus, Ada has come close to guaranteeing true portability: A program can be written for one computer with the near-certainty that it can be recompiled and run correctly on other machines. This alone makes Ada an important programming tool for big projects, bringing order to at least a portion of the turbulent world of computer languages.

The Indispensable Mediators

Converting a program written in a high-level language into the binary code that operates a computer requires painstaking attention to innumerable details, something computers, guided by translating software, do exceedingly well. Such translator programs fall into two categories: compilers and interpreters. A compiler translates the original high-level program into machine instructions and then stores the instructions without executing them; the compiled program can be recalled for use at any later time. An interpreter, in contrast, translates the high-level program into a set of intermediate commands, then immediately carries them out by sending appropriate machine instructions to the computer's central processing unit.

Each type of translation process has advantages and disadvantages. Programs that have been compiled usually run more quickly than those that must be interpreted; once translated, the compiled program has no further need of the compiler itself, and the computer does not have to juggle translation and execution. Programs written in languages that must be interpreted require the interpreter to be present in memory to make a translation each time the program is run.

However, an interpreter is useful for debugging as well as for translating programs that are subject to frequent changes; an altered program can be run immediately to see if it works. With a compiler, the entire program must be recompiled, a time-consuming requirement.

A characteristic of both interpreters and compilers is their reliance on the rules of the particular high-level language they are translating. In much the same way that grammatical rules govern human language, these rules regulate the work of the programmer, establishing the way the words and symbols used in the language may be combined to create complex expressions, and specifying such format features as spacing and punctuation. In the translator, this grammar is the basis for transforming the abstractions of the original program into the machine code that gets the job done.

Steps That Transform Written Programs

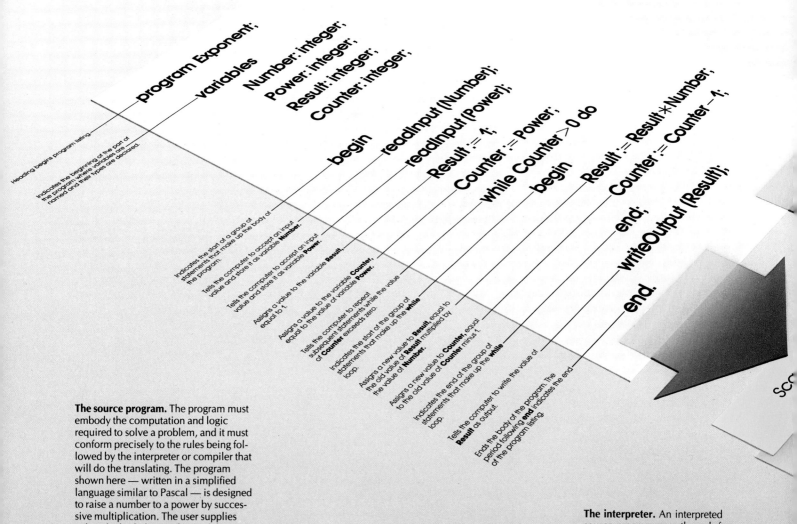

The following is the program shown in the diagram, in reading order:

```
program Exponent;
variables
    Number: integer;
    Power: integer;
    Result: integer;
    Counter: integer;
begin
    readInput (Number);
    readInput (Power);
    Result := 1;
    Counter := Power;
    while Counter > 0 do
    begin
        Result := Result * Number;
        Counter := Counter - 1;
    end;
    writeOutput (Result);
end.
```

Annotations (left to right):

- Heading begins program listing.
- Indicates the beginning of the part of the program where variables are named and their types are declared.
- Indicates the start of a group of statements that make up the body of the program.
- Tells the computer to accept an input value and store it as variable **Number**.
- Tells the computer to accept an input value and store it as variable **Power**.
- Assigns a value to the variable **Result**, equal to 1.
- Assigns a value to the variable **Counter**, equal to the value of variable **Power**.
- Tells the computer to repeat subsequent statements while the value of **Counter** exceeds zero.
- Indicates the start of the group of statements that make up the **while** loop.
- Assigns a new value to **Result**, equal to the old value of **Result** multiplied by the value of **Number**.
- Assigns a new value to **Counter**, equal to the old value of **Counter** minus 1.
- Indicates the end of the group of statements that make up the **while** loop.
- Tells the computer to write the value of **Result** as output.
- Ends the body of the program. The period following **end** indicates the end of the program listing.

The source program. The program must embody the computation and logic required to solve a problem, and it must conform precisely to the rules being followed by the interpreter or compiler that will do the translating. The program shown here — written in a simplified language similar to Pascal — is designed to raise a number to a power by successive multiplication. The user supplies values for both the number and the power; the program requires only that the values be positive integers.

The interpreter. An interpreted source program goes through four phases in translation. First, a scanner converts the source code into symbols the interpreter can understand. Then a parser arranges those symbols in a hierarchy reflecting the program's logic. A type checker analyzes the rearranged symbols to find programming errors. Finally, an executor program sends the computer's central processing unit a series of machine instructions to perform the operations specified by each symbol.

A high-level program begins as ordinary text, entered into the computer through a keyboard in the same way that a business letter would be. But the program, called the source program or source code, is more strictly bound by grammatical rules than ordinary human communication.

When the translator program (either an interpreter or a compiler) is instructed to begin working on the source code, a copy of the high-level program is brought into the computer's memory along with the translating program. The translator then begins to read the source code, character by character, working on it in several stages, as shown below. A different job is done at each stage, with the translator taking the transformed code from the preceding step, manipulating it and passing it on. If any of the programming language's grammatical rules are broken, the translator activates an error-handling mechanism that notifies the programmer of the mistake.

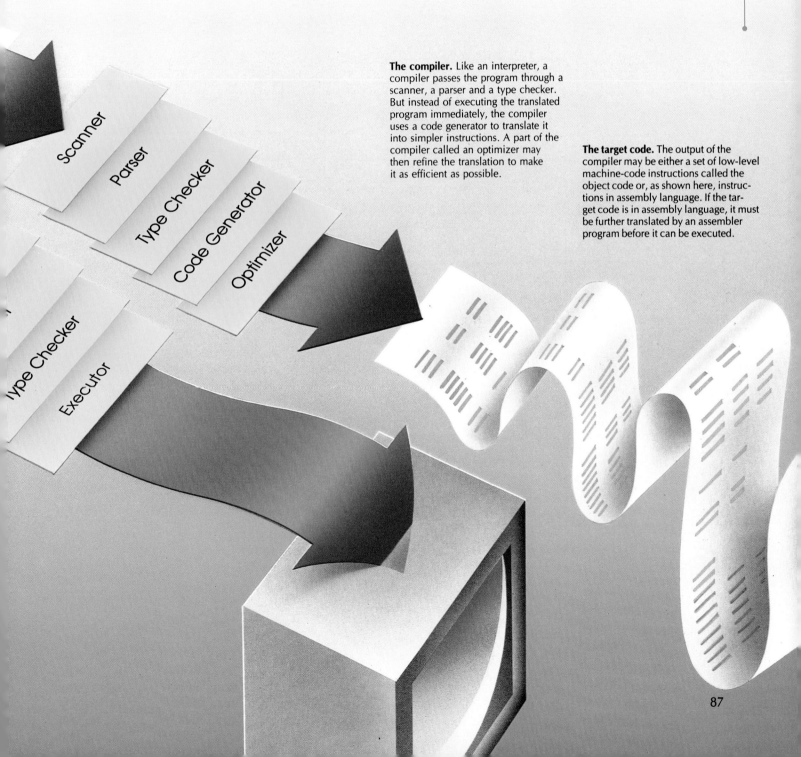

The compiler. Like an interpreter, a compiler passes the program through a scanner, a parser and a type checker. But instead of executing the translated program immediately, the compiler uses a code generator to translate it into simpler instructions. A part of the compiler called an optimizer may then refine the translation to make it as efficient as possible.

The target code. The output of the compiler may be either a set of low-level machine-code instructions called the object code or, as shown here, instructions in assembly language. If the target code is in assembly language, it must be further translated by an assembler program before it can be executed.

A First Glance at the Written Program

The job of the scanner is to make the source code intelligible to the rest of the translator program. Reading the characters of the source code individually, the scanner follows the grammatical rules of the programming language to organize the characters into groups and determine their meanings. For each meaningful group, the scanner generates a symbol called a token, which is sent to the next stage of the translator; the scanner's procedures allow it to work on only one token at a time. When the scanner produces the tokens, it discards the adjacent spacing and indentation of the source

The scanner uses grammatical rules to transform the characters of the source program into tokens — units that have meaning to the translator. The rules specify the exact meanings of tokens that stand for keywords, operators, numbers and punctuation. The meanings of identifier tokens, however, are established in the source program. The scanner sets up a symbol table *(above)*, assigning each identifier a label and leaving space for attributes to be filled in later.

program, which are of no further use to the translator.

Most of the tokens the scanner creates have a fixed meaning. Keywords — such as BEGIN, IF and END — refer to actions defined by the syntax of the programming language. Operators — such as + and := (which means "is assigned the value of") — refer to arithmetic, logic or data-storage operations. Numbers represent actual numerical values, such as 5 or 7. Punctuation marks help the translator understand the structure of the program.

Another kind of token, called an identifier, has no fixed meaning. Identifiers represent terms that are not defined by the rules of the language, such as the program's name or words selected by the programmer to represent variables and constants. The scanner attaches its own labels to these tokens to allow the translator to keep track of them, and lists them by name and label in a symbol table. Space is left in the table for other attributes of the identifiers that the translator will require. These attributes can be listed in the source program, and as the scanner encounters them, it associates them with their respective identifiers.

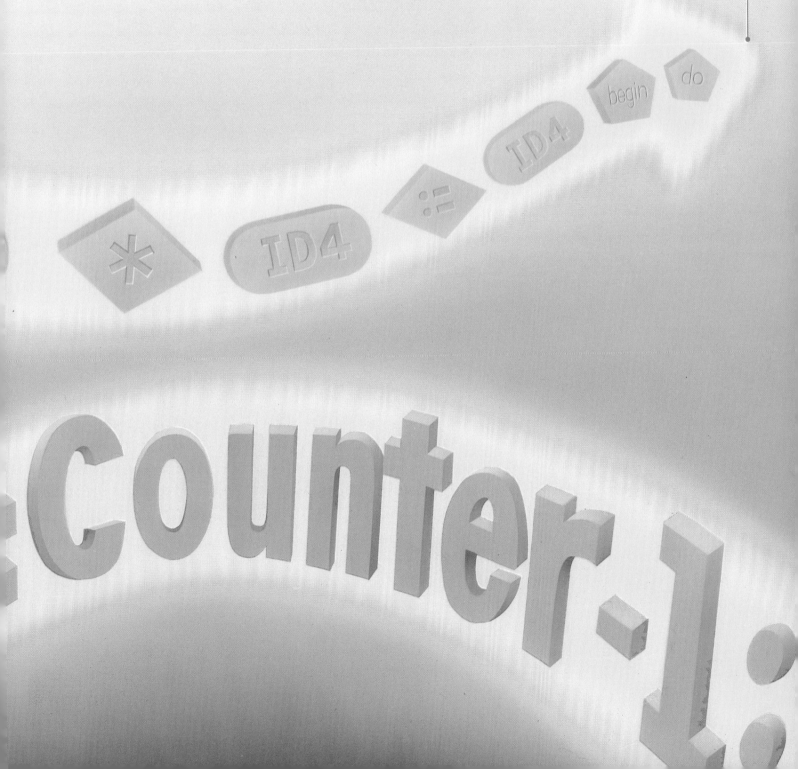

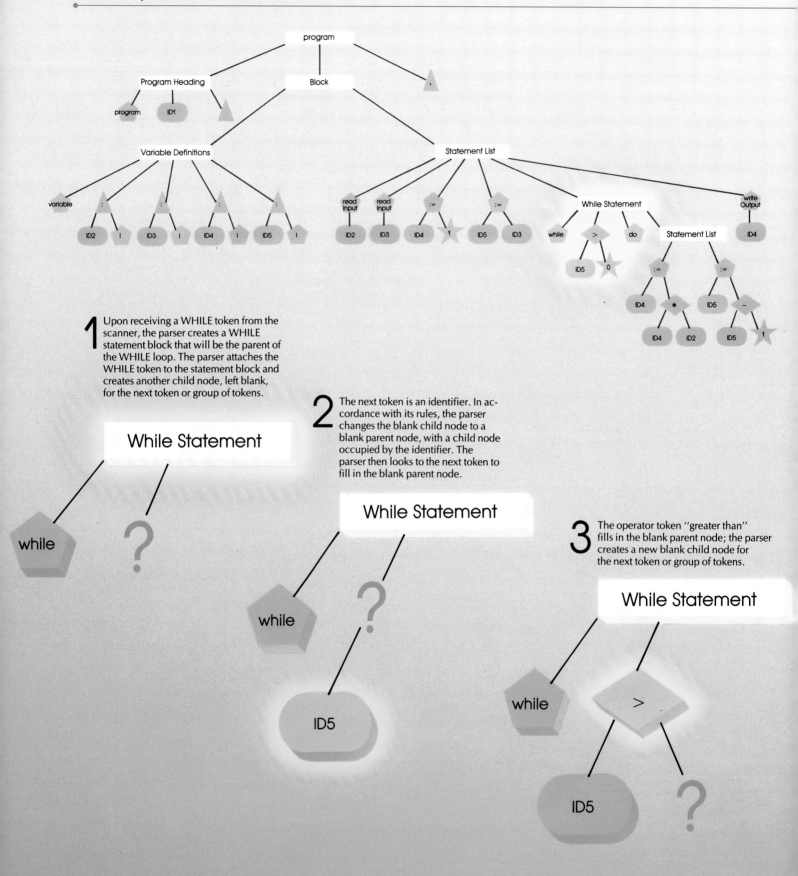

3

1 Upon receiving a WHILE token from the scanner, the parser creates a WHILE statement block that will be the parent of the WHILE loop. The parser attaches the WHILE token to the statement block and creates another child node, left blank, for the next token or group of tokens.

2 The next token is an identifier. In accordance with its rules, the parser changes the blank child node to a blank parent node, with a child node occupied by the identifier. The parser then looks to the next token to fill in the blank parent node.

3 The operator token "greater than" fills in the blank parent node; the parser creates a new blank child node for the next token or group of tokens.

Fitting Pieces on a Tree of Relations

The parser takes tokens as they emerge from the scanner and arranges them in a structure that allows the computer to decipher the logic of the program. This structure can be thought of as a hierarchical arrangement similar to a family tree *(right)*. The tokens may be parents, children or both. Groups of tokens that serve a common purpose are organized under statement blocks, which mark the major divisions of the program. The parse tree for the program EXPONENT is shown at left. The

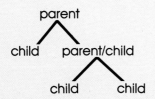

parser decides how to position each token on the tree by examining the meaning of the token, the tokens that have preceded it and, in some cases, the token immediately following it. An explicit set of rules governs tree building; a particular sequence of tokens can result in only one arrangement. The process is demonstrated below in the construction of the WHILE loop, which is highlighted at left in its complete form. If the parser encounters a sequence of tokens that does not fit its rules, it assumes that the program contains an error. In this situation, the translator sends the programmer an error message that may contain information on the type and location of the mistake.

4 The next token is a number; in this case, the parser's rule is to create another blank child node *(lower question mark)*. If the succeeding token is an operator, it will go in the parent node *(upper question mark)*, with the number as its child. If the succeeding token is not an operator, the number will occupy the first blank node and it will have no child.

5 The next token is a keyword, DO, so the number token fills the child node of the "greater than" operator. The DO token becomes a child of the WHILE statement block, and a new blank node is created for the next group of tokens. This node will in turn be filled by another statement block containing several layers of children *(complete tree, above left)*.

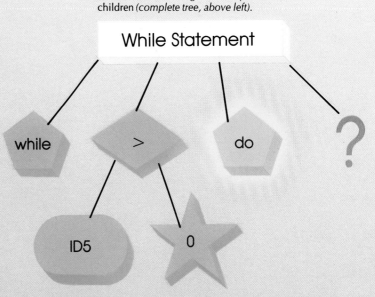

Type Checking to Detect Errors

After the parser organizes the tokens, the translator examines their collective as well as their individual meanings. This analysis is applied first to error checking, the process of looking for parts of the program that violate rules of the language. One of the most important kinds of error analysis is type

1 The section of the program where variables are declared is parsed like the rest of the program, so that each identifier is clearly linked with its attributes. In this program, all of the identifiers except the program name represent variables of the same type: integer.

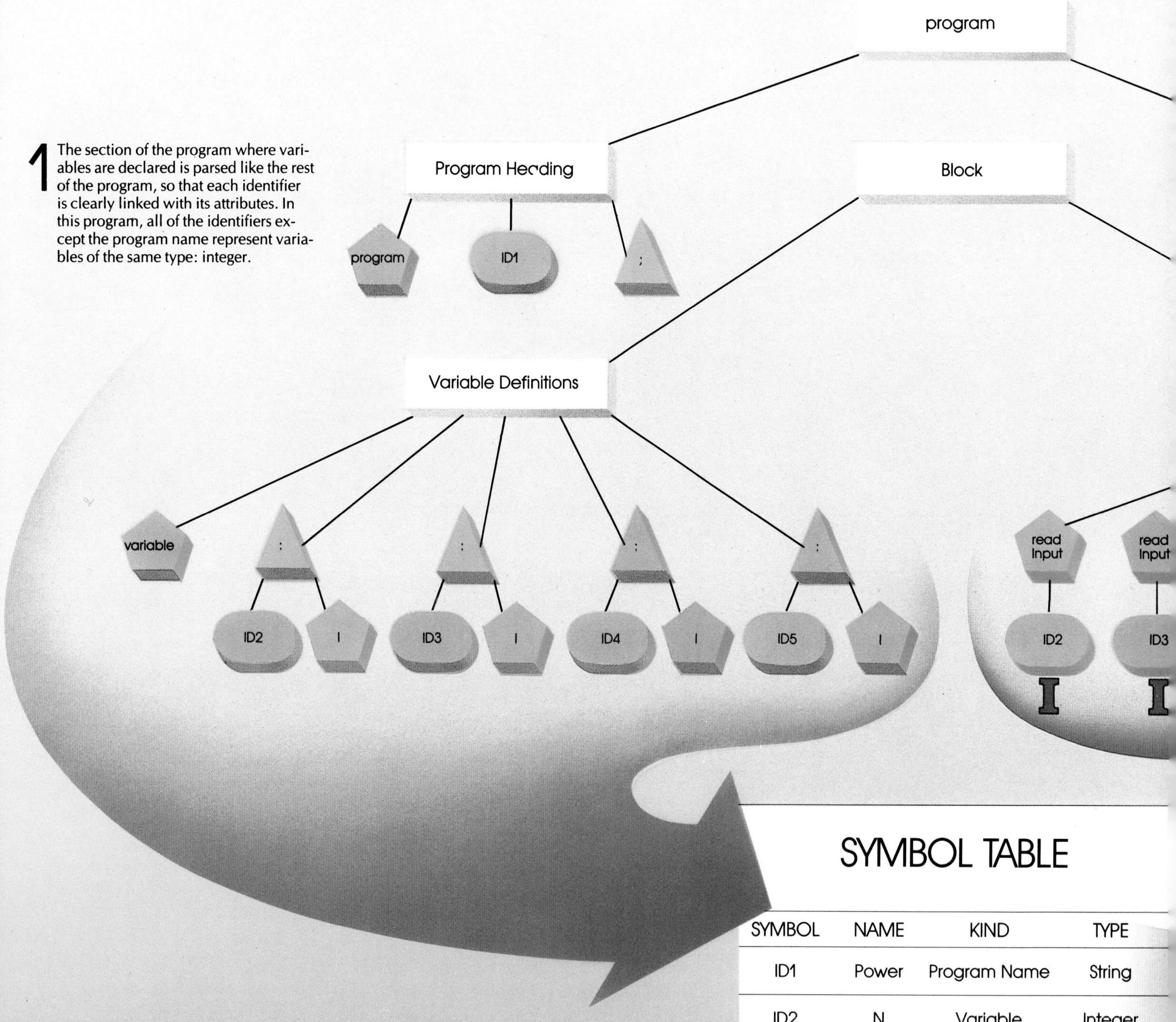

program

Program Heading

Block

program

ID1

;

Variable Definitions

variable

:

:

:

:

read Input

read Input

ID2

I

ID3

I

ID4

I

ID5

I

ID2

ID3

SYMBOL TABLE

SYMBOL	NAME	KIND	TYPE
ID1	Power	Program Name	String
ID2	N	Variable	Integer
ID3	P	Variable	Integer
ID4	Result	Variable	Integer
ID5	Counter	Variable	Integer

2 The translator uses the parsed variable declarations to fill in the blanks of the symbol table that was begun by the scanner. Each identifier is now associated with the variable or constant that it represents and with the type of its data.

checking. Many programming languages, including the one used here, require that a program explicitly declare data types *(pages 52-53)*. (In other languages, if the program does not provide this information, the translator must infer it from the context in which variables are used.) If the data types employed in an expression are incompatible *(box, right)*, the translated program would fail to work properly. By catching such errors during translation, the translator can improve the reliability of the program.

Type checking serves another important function, giving the translator information about tokens that it needs to begin generating code. For example, an operator such as the + character may act in different ways, and therefore require different coding, depending on the types of its children.

Dealing with Mismatched Types

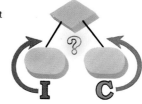

When two children of one parent have different types, the translator can follow a rule that allows the translation to continue. For instance, if one child's type is real number and the other's is integer, the rule might specify that the parent's type is real number. But other mismatches may have no reconciliation. Here, one child is integer type and the other is character type; there is no rule for this combination, and the translator sends an error message to the programmer.

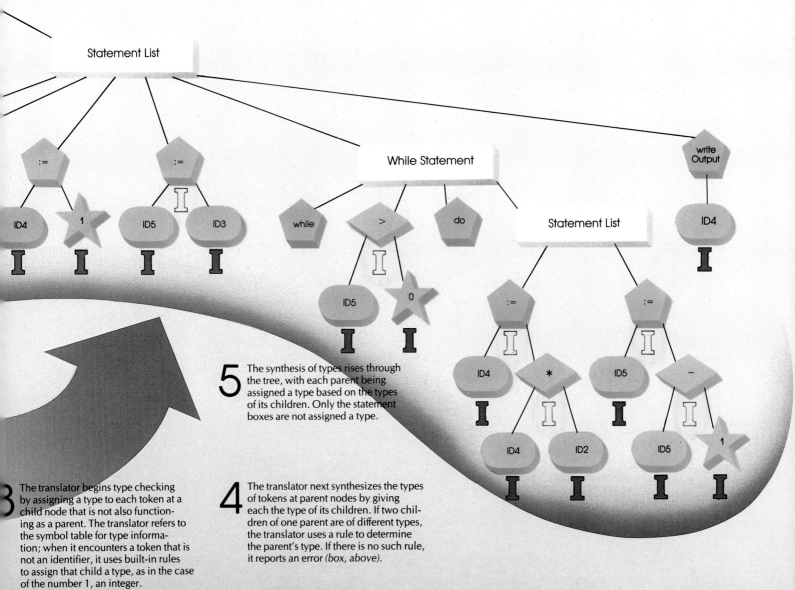

5 The synthesis of types rises through the tree, with each parent being assigned a type based on the types of its children. Only the statement boxes are not assigned a type.

3 The translator begins type checking by assigning a type to each token at a child node that is not also functioning as a parent. The translator refers to the symbol table for type information; when it encounters a token that is not an identifier, it uses built-in rules to assign that child a type, as in the case of the number 1, an integer.

4 The translator next synthesizes the types of tokens at parent nodes by giving each the type of its children. If two children of one parent are of different types, the translator uses a rule to determine the parent's type. If there is no such rule, it reports an error *(box, above)*.

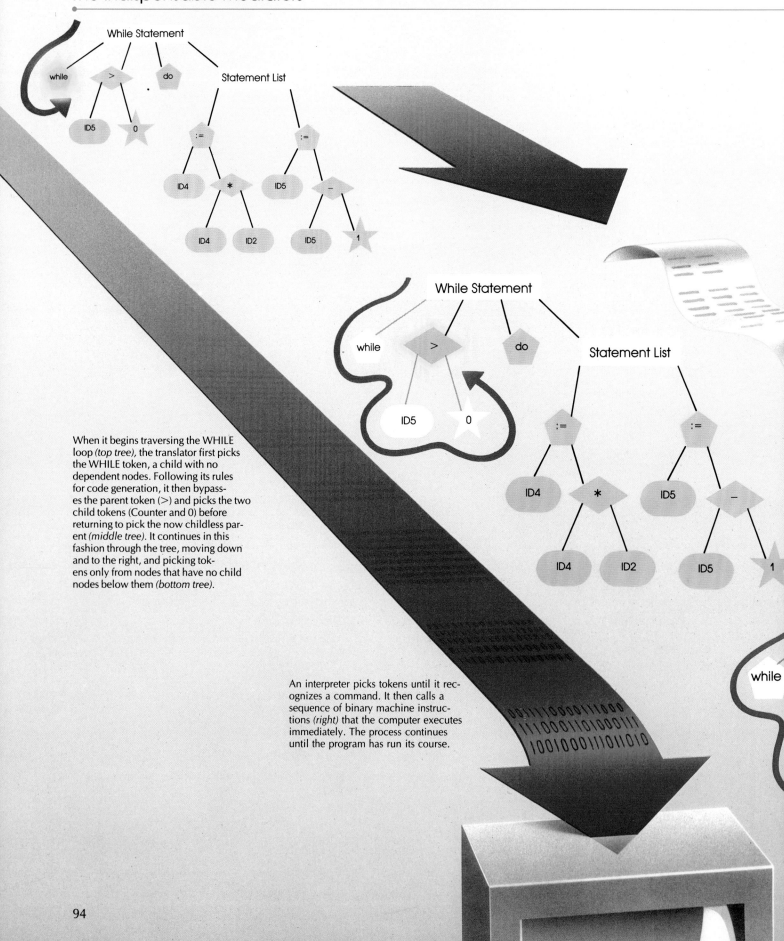

When it begins traversing the WHILE loop *(top tree)*, the translator first picks the WHILE token, a child with no dependent nodes. Following its rules for code generation, it then bypasses the parent token (>) and picks the two child tokens (Counter and 0) before returning to pick the now childless parent *(middle tree)*. It continues in this fashion through the tree, moving down and to the right, and picking tokens only from nodes that have no child nodes below them *(bottom tree)*.

An interpreter picks tokens until it recognizes a command. It then calls a sequence of binary machine instructions *(right)* that the computer executes immediately. The process continues until the program has run its course.

Dismantling the Tree to Make Instructions

Once the tree of tokens is complete, the translator program performs its most critical task: It turns tokens into the sequences of machine instructions that will direct the computer. It does this by means of a process known as traversing the tree. The translator moves through the parse tree taking tokens from their nodes in a prescribed order.

As with the rest of the translation process, traversing the tree is governed by the rules of the language used to write the source program. The translator shown here begins at the top left of the tree and moves down and to the right around the tree's perimeter. When it encounters a token at a parent node, it bypasses the node, continuing down the tree until it encounters a child node that has no subsidiary nodes of its own. It then picks the token at that node and continues, eventually picking all the children at the lowest level of that branch. This makes the former parent nodes at the next-higher level into child nodes, which can now be picked.

A compiler traverses the tree for the entire program. When it has gathered enough tokens to form a logical command, it produces the instructions corresponding to that command and continues through the tree. The instructions the compiler generates are then stored by the computer for later execution or manipulation. An interpreter, in contrast, does not store its results, but passes machine instructions directly to the computer for execution.

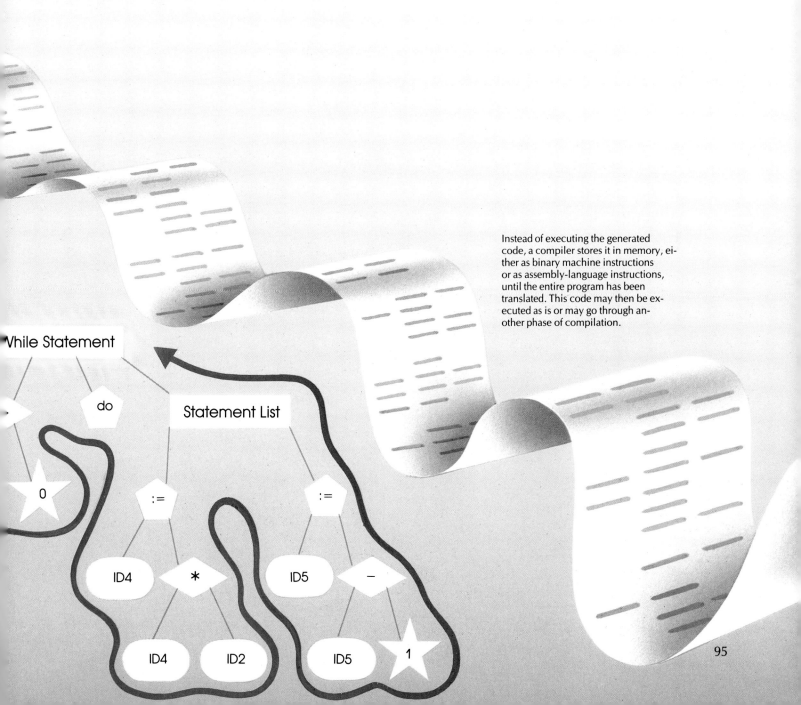

Instead of executing the generated code, a compiler stores it in memory, either as binary machine instructions or as assembly-language instructions, until the entire program has been translated. This code may then be executed as is or may go through another phase of compilation.

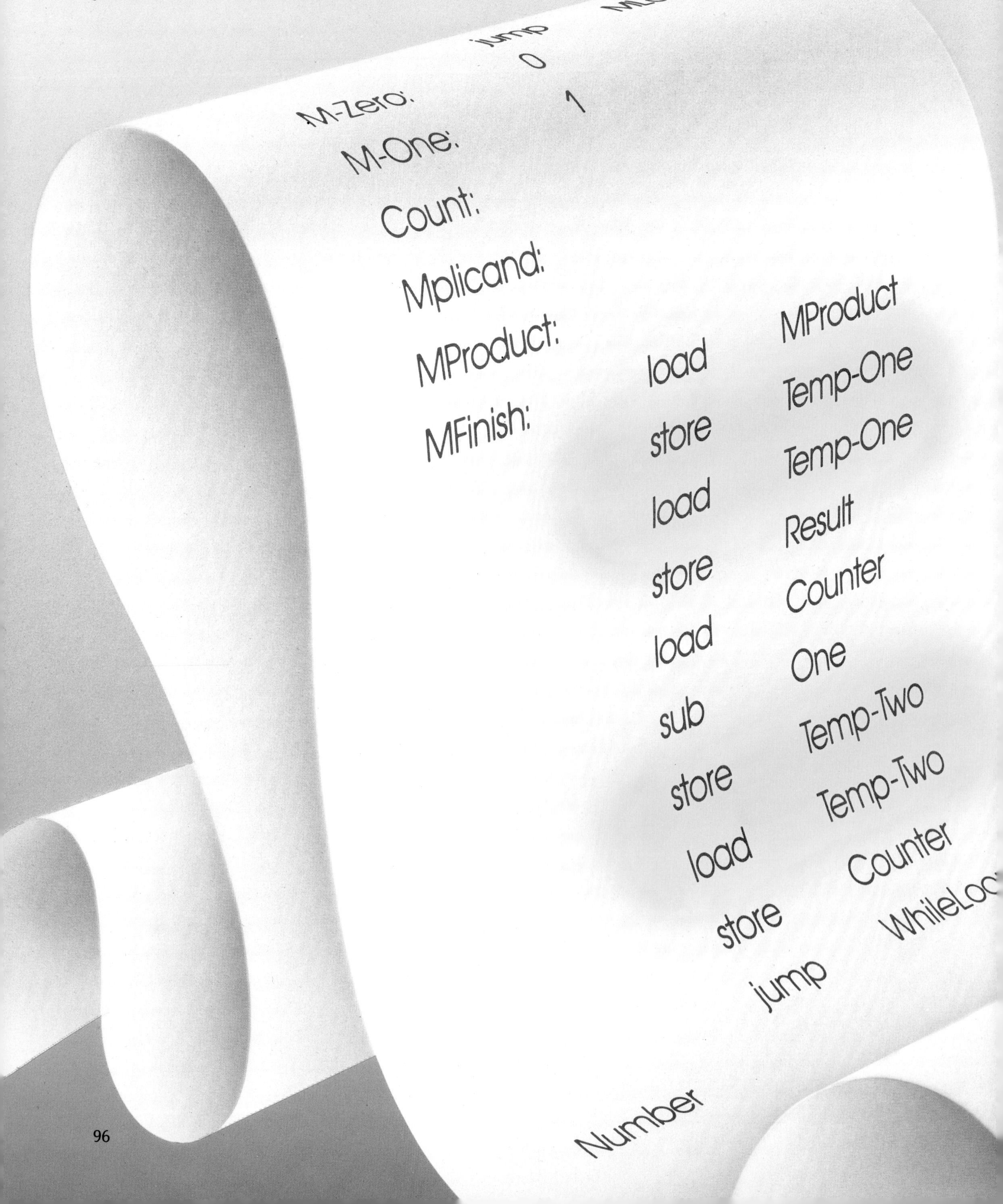

jump   MLoop

M-Zero: 0

M-One: 1

Count:

Mplicand:

MProduct:

MFinish:

```
            load    MProduct
            store   Temp-One
            load    Temp-One
            store   Result
            load    Counter
            sub     One
            store   Temp-Two
            load    Temp-Two
            store   Counter
            jump    WhileLoo
```

Number

Fine-Tuning for Efficient Code

A translator is designed to work only on the material at hand; it can look neither forward to the code it is about to generate nor backward to the code it has already created. The resulting machine instructions may therefore be redundant or poorly organized — or both. Although an interpreter can do nothing about this, a compiler is equipped with a tool that can eliminate these inefficiencies.

The last stage of the compiler, called the optimizer, can search the target code for places where the program can be improved. The optimizer has two basic and sometimes conflicting goals: to shorten the program so that it occupies less space in memory, and to reorganize the program so that it will run faster when it is executed. One of the optimizer's most fundamental tasks is to find and remove extraneous commands, as illustrated here with part of the target code for the program EXPONENT. At two places in this section of the program, the compiler has generated machine instructions that, in effect, cancel each other out. By eliminating both pairs of commands, the optimizer simultaneously produces both a shorter program and a faster execution time.

Other kinds of optimization require sophisticated computation and may greatly lengthen the compilation process. Some compilers therefore make a compromise, paying close attention only to those parts of the target code — such as loops and procedures — that are likely to be heavily used when the program is executed. The optimizer can then fine-tune the target code in these sections to gain improvements in execution time without paying too high a price in compilation time.

In the portion of the assembly-language program shown here, the optimizer finds two pairs of superfluous commands. In each case, the computer is told to store the contents of the accumulator, then to return the same information to the accumulator unchanged. The optimizer can eliminate both pairs to shorten the target program without changing its meaning.

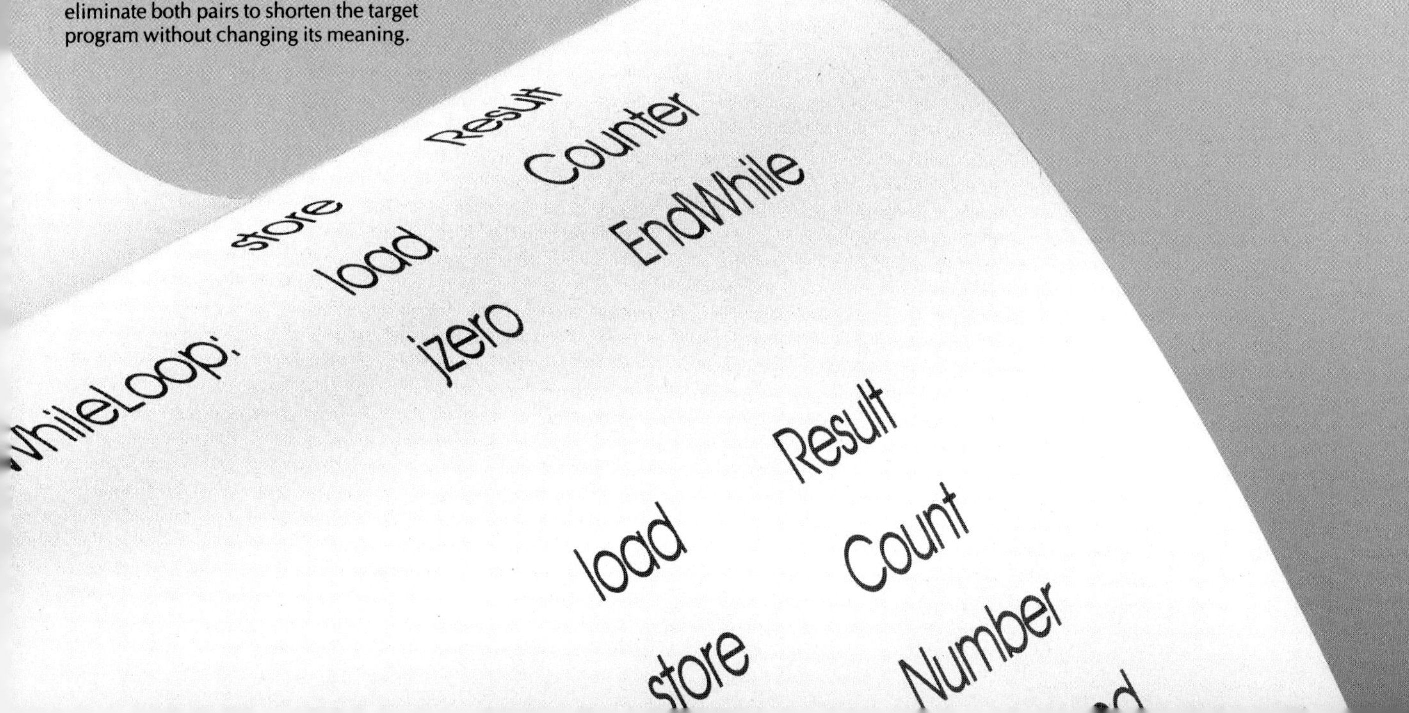

WhileLoop:

store Result

load Counter

jzero EndWhile

load Result

store Count

Number

Programming Comes Home

In 1964, a programmer in Minneapolis named Robert L. Albrecht was intrigued by word of the new language called BASIC that had been introduced recently at Dartmouth College. As both its acronym and full name — Beginner's All-Purpose Symbolic Instruction Code — suggest, the language was intended for novices; a person with no computer experience could learn to use it in only a few hours. Furthermore, BASIC had been designed to run on a time-sharing system for Dartmouth's General Electric 225 computer, meaning that several students could interact with the machine at the same time. Instead of handing their punched-card programs over to trained computer operators and waiting as much as a day for processing (to say nothing of the two or three weeks it would take to get their programs debugged), students could sit at individual terminals and hone their programming skills through trial-and-error and immediate feedback. "BASIC gave a kind of access to computers that had never existed before," said Albrecht later. "It took computing out of the realm of the high priests."

Bob Albrecht himself was part of that elite company of computer programmers, operators and engineers who controlled access to the early computers. The son of a prosperous Iowa turkey and cattle farmer, he majored in physics and applied mathematics at the University of Minnesota and became enthralled by computers in 1955 while working in the aeronautical division of Minneapolis-Honeywell. He taught himself to program in machine code on the company's IBM 650 and drew immense satisfaction from communicating to others the joy he found in computing. Someday, he hoped, a revolution in technology would bring forth small, affordable computers that would allow people at large to write their own programs.

In 1962, as a senior applications analyst for Control Data in Denver, Albrecht persuaded his employer and the local school board to let him spread the computer gospel in Denver's high schools. Loading a refrigerator-size Control Data 160 minicomputer into his station wagon, he traveled from school to school with what he called "a modern-day medicine show," enlisting students he had trained in computing as barkers to drum up enthusiasm for classes in FORTRAN. The following year, Control Data transferred him to its Minneapolis headquarters as a full-time education specialist. There, he devised a simplified version of FORTRAN for students — BEFORTRAN, he called it (pointing out later that the dialect actually foreshadowed BASIC, which also was derived from FORTRAN).

Once Albrecht discovered BASIC, he became an instant convert and evangelist. He even had buttons made up proclaiming his formation of SHAFT — the Society to Help Abolish FORTRAN Teaching. Albrecht soon left corporate employment to devote himself to his crusade. He started writing the first of nearly a dozen books on BASIC that he would either author or co-author. And, as a member of the computer committee of the National Council of Teachers of Mathematics, he lobbied successfully to have the

The personal-computer boom of the late 1970s meant renewed popularity for languages such as BASIC, Pascal and traditional assembly language as thousands of computer enthusiasts began programming in their own homes.

group recommend BASIC as the teaching language for secondary schools.

The crusade reached full swing in 1966 when, at the age of 36, Albrecht migrated to northern California and plunged into the flourishing counterculture in San Francisco. He found himself among a like-minded community of dropouts from data processing — programmers and engineers who wanted to put the power of the computer into everybody's hands.

COMPUTING AT 50 CENTS AN HOUR

In the early 1970s, Albrecht launched Dymax, a publishing company that produced a series of instructional books on BASIC, including one of his own. He also started a walk-in computer center that would eventually be housed in a former corner drugstore in Menlo Park, about 40 miles south of San Francisco. The People's Computer Center possessed a PDP-8 minicomputer, provided by the Digital Equipment Corporation (DEC) in exchange for Albrecht's promise to write a book about programming the PDP-8 in BASIC. The center also boasted a terminal with telephone access to a computer at nearby Hewlett-Packard; a time-sharing company donated the computer time. For a fee of only 50 cents an hour, Albrecht told a reporter, "people can walk in like they do to a bowling alley or penny arcade and find out how to have fun with computers." The center also offered free classes in BASIC, which attracted teenagers, housewives and even a couple of businessmen, who were hoping to make a killing in the market by developing programs that would predict stock prices. Programming in BASIC was easier than ever. Interpreters had generally replaced the compiler used for the original Dartmouth BASIC. By translating the program line by line instead of all at once, as the compiler did, the new BASIC interpreters made the language even more interactive; users could debug their programs as they went.

At about this time, Albrecht also launched a bimonthly tabloid — the *People's Computer Company* — which became a kind of bulletin board for nonestablishment computing. It listed programs in BASIC, told where to buy inexpensive hardware and carried hacker gossip — all in columns of type so hurriedly thrown together they were almost always out of plumb. The paper had been heralding the coming revolution in small computers for more than two years when the first substantial token of that revolution finally arrived in 1975 — by mail.

The Altair 8800, a blue metal box mounted with toggle switches and a bank of flashing lights, was the first affordable microcomputer — $397 in kit form, $498 assembled. Albrecht received one of the very first models produced by its New Mexico manufacturer, Micro Instrumentation and Telemetry Systems (MITS). Though Albrecht and his colleagues were ecstatic and devoted page after page in their paper to the Altair, the little blue box clearly left a lot to be desired. It had no keyboard, no CRT screen, no means of permanent storage and — at 256 bytes — scarcely enough memory to hold a paragraph's worth of information. The memory could be increased, but even so, the first Altairs came with no programs and no translator for any high-level language to write them in. The only language a programmer could use was the computer's native machine code.

What the Altair needed, Albrecht realized at once, was BASIC. Translators for mainframe languages such as FORTRAN and COBOL required far too much memory. Even BASIC would have to be modified before an interpreter could be shoehorned in. Seeking what he called "a stripped-down version" of BASIC,

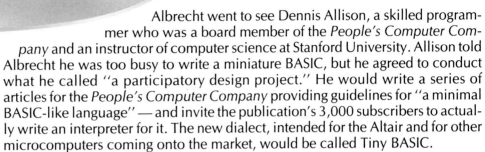

Albrecht went to see Dennis Allison, a skilled programmer who was a board member of the *People's Computer Company* and an instructor of computer science at Stanford University. Allison told Albrecht he was too busy to write a miniature BASIC, but he agreed to conduct what he called "a participatory design project." He would write a series of articles for the *People's Computer Company* providing guidelines for "a minimal BASIC-like language" — and invite the publication's 3,000 subscribers to actually write an interpreter for it. The new dialect, intended for the Altair and for other microcomputers coming onto the market, would be called Tiny BASIC.

In his first article, Allison set the tone by telling readers: "Pretend you are seven years old and don't care much about floating-point arithmetic (what's that?), logarithms, sines, matrix inversion, nuclear-reactor calculations and stuff like that." In late 1975, less than a month after Allison's final article appeared, the first Tiny BASIC interpreter arrived in the mail. It consisted of about 20 pages of octal code from two Texas hobbyists, Dick Whipple and John Arnold, who described themselves as "the Tyler Branch of the North Texas Computer Club." Whipple, who taught college mathematics and physics, and Arnold, a high-school math teacher, had laboriously flipped toggle switches on the Altair for nearly three hours to load in a separate machine-code program that would allow them to use a keyboard. They then entered some 2,000 octal-code instructions. (In the course of this project, the two Texans bought memory boards from MITS to increase the machine's capacity to four kilobytes.) With the interpreter in memory, the Altair had responded handsomely to commands entered in Tiny BASIC — until a power failure erased the contents of the computer's memory, leaving them only the printed octal listing to show for their work.

Albrecht published news of the Texans' Tiny BASIC in the December issue of *People's Computer Company*, promising to send interested readers a copy of the octal code, which would enable them to write Tiny BASIC programs for their machines. Expecting a dozen or so responses, he was deluged by several hundred. Meanwhile, other versions of Tiny BASIC were pouring in.

THE NAME GAME
To deal with the obvious demand, Albrecht and Allison decided to publish a new magazine devoted solely to Tiny BASIC. They left the naming of the publication to their production coordinator, Eric Bakalinsky, who proceeded to work his way toward a suitable title by asking some questions and freely interpreting the answers: What was Tiny BASIC, anyway? Bakalinsky asked a colleague. He was told it was an "exercise in developing a language." Bakalinsky translated this as "calisthenics." Who was responsible for it? he asked. Dennis Allison and Bob Albrecht. He compressed their names into "Dobb." What was its goal? To save bytes of information in the computer's memory — a concept that in Bakalinsky's mind turned into an image of an orthodontist curing a patient's "overbyte." Hence, the name of the new magazine emerged: *Dr. Dobb's Journal of Tiny BASIC Calisthenics & Orthodontia: Running Light without Overbyte.*

The name was modified slightly before the first issue, with the word "Computer" replacing "Tiny BASIC." This reflected the desire of the new editor, Jim Warren, to broaden the magazine's scope so that it would serve as an "intellectual rabble-rouser" and include information about "free and very inexpensive software" besides Tiny BASIC. Under Warren's irreverent stewardship, the magazine published an eclectic range of microcomputer news, from projects for home computers to occasional weighty essays on improved methods of programming. It also carried new versions of Tiny BASIC submitted by readers. Li-Chen Wang, a Stanford graduate student, for example, came up with Palo Alto Tiny BASIC, which proved to be one of the most popular dialects.

Authors of these dialects released them to the public domain, where they were free for the copying. But other readers took a more commercial tack. Tom Pittman, a member of the Homebrew Computer Club, which had been founded by a handful of regulars from Albrecht's walk-in center, wrote a Tiny BASIC interpreter in 1975 for several new microcomputers that were built around the Motorola 6800 chip. He sold the interpreter to a manufacturer for $3,500 — but only on the condition that he could maintain his own marketing rights. Pittman, a shy, middle-aged hacker, had no intention of going into business. He merely wanted to prove that good software could be designed and sold for a reasonable price.

By now MITS, the manufacturer of the Altair, was marketing its own version of BASIC for $500 (unless the purchaser bought additional memory boards from the company; the price for the BASIC software would then drop to $150). This version had been written in the spring of 1975, about the same time Albrecht launched the Tiny BASIC project, by Harvard freshman Bill Gates and his friend Paul Allen, a young Honeywell programmer. The pair then sold it to MITS on a per-copy royalty basis. Pittman's colleagues in the Homebrew Computer Club resented the high price of Altair BASIC, insisting that software ought to be free. ("In those days we thought everything should be free," Albrecht remarked later.) Someone — probably one of the Homebrewers — pirated the Altair program and distributed free copies, setting off a furor that rocked the computer community.

As a test of whether his fellow hackers would refrain from pirating software if it were reasonably priced, Pittman offered hobbyists his Tiny BASIC interpreter, coded on punched paper tape, for a mere five dollars. The response was so gratifying that Pittman announced his intention to write a tiny FORTRAN for microcomputers and sell it for $25. But he gave up the enterprise after suffering a domestic setback all too familiar to devoted hackers. "My computer widow left me," he explained. "She decided she didn't want to be married to an addict."

THE BURGEONING OF BASIC

As the 1970s drew to a close, so did the story of Altair and Tiny BASIC. Microcomputers were entering the market fully assembled, with larger memories that could accommodate larger BASIC dialects. Some manufacturers wired interpreters for their own versions of BASIC into the machines themselves, embedding them in ROM, the computer's so-called read-only, or permanent, memory. So many variations appeared — often tailored to take advantage of the features of a particular microcomputer — that designers began to speak of BASIC as a class of languages rather than as a single language with dialects. Soon the most popular version of all was MBASIC (a direct descendant of Altair BASIC), which Gates and Allen had used to launch their highly successful Microsoft Corporation.

Largely because of the enterprise of Gates and Allen, the tireless promotion of Bob Albrecht and the enthusiasm of all the little-known designers of home-grown Tiny BASICs, the language in its many versions came to dominate microcomputer programming. By the mid-1980s, several million people in the United States and abroad were conversant with BASIC, and a majority of them had learned it on personal computers.

Two who had decidedly mixed feelings about BASIC's phenomenal success were the language's original designers, John Kemeny and Thomas Kurtz of Dartmouth College. They were fiercely proud of BASIC's catalytic role "in helping open computers up to the masses," as Kemeny put it, but they were also dismayed by what their language had become. "The first microcomputers had very limited memories, so that implementors had to make a number of compromises—some of which were most unfortunate," Kemeny and Kurtz wrote in 1985. "Many of these compromises became features of the language and were kept when the original reasons for compromising had disappeared."

As a result, the many versions of BASIC were not portable from machine to machine. And there were other problems with the language as well. For one, many computer scientists viewed the language with some disdain. Britain's C.A.R. Hoare, for example, likened programming in BASIC to playing the piano with two fingers: The beginner makes rapid progress through the first easy tunes, but then runs into enormous difficulty. BASIC lends itself to brief, simple programs but not to long, complex ones, largely because the original language lacked structure. With the GOTO statement, for instance, control could shift from one part of a program to another, resulting in what was often referred to as "spaghetti code." This lack of structure led some colleges and high schools to abandon BASIC as the language for teaching programming and to take up Niklaus Wirth's more rigorously structured Pascal in its stead.

SHAPING A TRUE STANDARD

Over the years, Kemeny and Kurtz periodically revised the original Dartmouth version of BASIC, even replacing the GOTO statement with more sophisticated control structures. But having put BASIC in the public domain at the outset, they had no power over what happened to it beyond the Dartmouth campus. To remedy this, Kemeny and Kurtz collaborated in 1984 on a microcomputer version of BASIC that was intended to comply with BASIC standards developed by the American National Standards Institute (ANSI). This major overhaul incorporated principles of structured programming and used a combination interpreter-compiler to translate programs into machine code. The hybrid translator not only revealed errors immediately but was designed to make programs easily transportable between different makes and models of machines. In choosing a name for the new and definitive version of their 20-year-old language, Kemeny and Kurtz made clear their attitude toward other dialects: They called it True BASIC.

Kemeny and Kurtz had a fellow victim of success in Pascal inventor Niklaus Wirth. By the late 1970s, Wirth's highly structured language had gained wide acceptance in the university classroom. But as software developers attempted to adapt Pascal to microcomputers and other commercial purposes, the language suffered some drastic changes. Because Wirth had originally designed Pascal to teach programming to students, it contained few provisions for input/output and other features essential to practical programming. Consequently, more and more extensions were added to Pascal compilers to make the language useful outside the academic setting — resulting in the creation of different dialects.

Wirth disavowed all the new dialects, issuing, in 1977, this high-minded credo: "If a language proves to be only marginally suitable for some application that was obviously not envisaged by its originator, we should muster the courage to build a new, truly adequate tool, instead of just grafting a fix onto the existing one."

In fact, Wirth was doing exactly that. In 1981 he announced Modula-2, a language he had forged to replace Pascal for general-purpose applications. Like Ada, Modula-2 expanded upon Pascal in a number of ways, most notably by providing for large and complex programs that could be composed in separate, self-contained modules and then fitted together. But during the early 1980s, while software companies sought to write compilers for Modula-2 that would allow the language to be used on microcomputers, an extraordinary thing happened to Pascal.

Prior to that period, various Pascal compilers for microcomputers had enjoyed only lukewarm commercial success because, in addition to being costly, they tended to occupy too much memory or disk space and worked at snail-like speeds. Then a former student of Wirth's came up with a compiler for micros he called Turbo Pascal. It was compact, lightning-fast and remarkably inexpensive.

THE JAZZ MAN

Turbo Pascal's developer was a self-styled "crazy Frenchman" named Philippe Kahn. A native of Paris — his German-born father was a mechanical engineer, his French mother an independent film maker — Kahn studied for a time in Zurich, where he enrolled in Wirth's introductory course in Pascal. He returned home to take the French equivalent of a Ph.D. in mathematics, paying his way partly by playing the saxophone at night in jazz clubs.

Kahn taught mathematics at the university level for a while. He was interested in computers only for their help in solving problems and proving theorems. Then he got his first microcomputer. "I discovered with my Apple II the mystique of Silicon Valley," he said later. For Kahn, some of that mystique centered on the fortune the Apple II was making for its creators, Steven Jobs and Stephen Wozniak. Along with two friends, he began earning money on a modest scale by writing microcomputer applications programs in Pascal; dissatisfaction with the available Pascal compilers led Kahn to develop Turbo Pascal. In 1982, with that program and $2,000 in his pocket, he left France for California.

In the beginning, Kahn could not even get a job there. Traveling on a tourist visa, he lacked a so-called green card, the government permit he needed to work in the United States. In desperation, he decided to gamble on Turbo Pascal and start his own software company. He called it Borland International, a name inspired by a TV commercial featuring a former astronaut with a similar name, Frank Borman, who was then board chairman of Eastern Airlines. Kahn thought the name had "an all-American sound to it" — a suitable cover for an alien in business illegally.

Despite the grand name, venture capitalists found little in Kahn's organization to inspire confidence. Kahn's associates in the new enterprise included such other high-tech novices as a former owner of a Japanese restaurant, who once sold sesame-seed salad dressing by mail, and a cocktail waitress working on her

Flourishing the saxophone he once played for a living, computer entrepreneur Philippe Kahn soaks his feet in the family-size hot tub he purchased with profits from sales of Turbo Pascal, the compact, low-priced compiler he released in 1983. Turbo Pascal sold more than a quarter of a million copies in its first two years on the market, becoming the standard version of Pascal for microcomputers.

Ph.D. in psychology. Unable to raise a dollar from conventional investment sources, Kahn put together a modest $20,000 stake from members of his own family. In March 1984 he set up shop in a two-room office above an auto-repair garage in Scotts Valley, 24 miles southwest of San Jose. "It was a Jaguar garage," Kahn remembers, "which gave it a little class." By staging what he called a "sting operation" — having friends act as secretaries and pretend to be taking calls from overseas — Kahn persuaded a salesman from a popular computer magazine to run a full-page advertisement for Turbo Pascal on credit.

Kahn realized that the ad might be his one shot at the market, and he made the most of it. The young émigré had read a book about mail-order sales that recommended using garish colors to catch the readers' attention; so he made sure his ad was done in bold greens, blues and pink. He recalled that "the book also said if you want to generate an impulse buy, the product has to cost less than $50." So he priced his sophisticated compiler and program editor at $49.95. It was a rock-bottom price; other systems were selling for up to 10 times that much.

The ad was a stroke of marketing genius. In the first month alone, it garnered $150,000 worth of orders, so many that the local banks suspected Kahn of mail fraud and initially refused to cash the flood of checks and credit card slips. But the orders kept rolling in, spurred by reviews in computer publications that likened Turbo Pascal's convenience in writing short programs to that of the old stand-by, BASIC. Experts also praised the speed of Kahn's compiler, which ran many times faster than its competitors.

Turbo Pascal sold no fewer than 300,000 copies in its first two years on the market, rising to the top of sales charts for all microcomputer languages. Just as a version of BASIC had fueled the rise of Microsoft a decade earlier, Turbo Pascal almost overnight catapulted Borland International into the ranks of major software companies. In 1985, Kahn threw a $45,000 party for 600 Borland employees and their guests. Presiding over the extravaganza, he wrapped his considerable girth in a purple-and-gold toga, wreathed his hair in grape leaves and saluted success at the age of 33 with a few riffs on his saxophone.

A NICHE IN THE MICRO WORLD

Many other languages originally designed for mainframes or minicomputers have been adapted for personal computers. LISP, the principal language in artificial-intelligence research, for example, has done fairly well because it allows programs to be written quickly and revised frequently — the essence of most microcomputer programming. Similarly, Bell Labs' C is widely used by professionals in writing applications programs for small computers.

Classics such as FORTRAN and COBOL, in contrast, failed to catch on even as microcomputers attained the memory size to cope with them. One reason was a lack of fast compilers. Another was that their strong suits — FORTRAN's aptitude for the lengthy number-manipulation tasks required in such applications as nuclear physics or engineering, and COBOL's ease in dealing with enormous quantities of simple data, such as employee records — were simply irrelevant to the programming needs of most personal-computer users.

But one language that had seemed destined for relative obscurity on larger computers did find new life during the microcomputer revolution. Named

FORTH, it slowly gained popularity largely through the grassroots efforts of individual enthusiasts. FORTH's designer, Charles H. Moore, maintained that he had not even set out to create a new language. Rather, he had developed FORTH gradually over the years as a way of increasing his own productivity. "The traditional languages were not providing the power, ease or flexibility that I wanted," he later explained. "I figured that in 40 years a very good programmer could write 40 programs. And I wanted to write *more* programs than that. There were things out in the world to be done, and I wanted a tool to help me do them."

A native of Michigan and a 1960 graduate of M.I.T., where he majored in physics, Moore began developing elements of FORTH in the early 1960s while writing programs at the Stanford Linear Accelerator Center in California. One element was compactness; FORTH's notation is so terse that certain keywords are no more than punctuation marks. Another feature, unusual in any language, is that FORTH is easy to extend: A programmer can simply define new keywords or commands in terms of old ones, thus tailoring the language's set of commands to almost any application.

By the late 1960s, when Moore was programming for a private company in upstate New York, these ideas had coalesced sufficiently to warrant calling them a language. Moore wanted to name his creation FOURTH because it seemed to him so powerful that it amounted to a generational leap beyond languages for the so-called third generation of computers then in use. (The completed language increased his own productivity by a factor of 10, he said.) But the IBM 1130 on which he was working limited the length of identifiers to five characters, so he abridged the name to FORTH, which he later conceded was "a nicer play on words anyway."

TUNING IN THE HEAVENS
The first significant application of FORTH occurred during the early 1970s, while Moore was with the National Radio Astronomy Observatory (NRAO) in Arizona. In collaboration with Elizabeth Rather, who managed software for NRAO in Tucson, he used the language to write a series of programs for a system of minicomputers that, among other things, controlled the real-time positioning of the 36-foot radio telescope at the observatory at Kitt Peak *(right)*. The programs and system proved so successful that in 1973 Moore, Rather and their boss at the observatory, Ned Conklin, went into business for themselves. Their new company, FORTH Inc., marketed systems not only for observatories but also for other specialized applications requiring real-time process control, such as the computer-operated video cameras on the submersible sled that located the wreck of the *Titanic* in 1985.

Though the company showed little interest in the personal-computer market—during the late 1970s its least-expensive system sold for $2,000—FORTH inspired remarkable fervor among some microcomputer hobbyists. One early disciple was a young Silicon Valley software engineer named Kim Harris. At a FORTH Inc. seminar, he watched in awe while, in a period of just 15 minutes, one of the demonstrators developed a simple program to play computer music. Harris knew a skilled hobbyist who had been laboring for more than a year to produce a similar program in assembly language. "It was like a religious miracle," Harris would recall, "and I saw it myself."

In 1977, Harris teamed with four other young converts to form the FORTH Interest Group (FIG) and set about developing a low-cost FORTH system for home hobbyists. The five founders and seven volunteers obtained an early public-domain interpreter for the language from the observatory and worked nights and weekends for more than six months to create a simplified interpreter for personal computers. The result, FIG-FORTH, was sold at cost for about $20. Other microcomputer versions of FORTH ultimately became available from commercial vendors, but FIG-FORTH dominated the home hobbyist field. FIG itself, meanwhile, grew to a membership of some 4,000 people in a score of countries.

FORTH is difficult to master and almost impossible for anyone except FORTH users to read. But its adherents say the language gives them increased power over the computer — the way a manual transmission makes an automobile more responsive to the driver. "A language like FORTH is a hacker's paradise," one enthusiast has observed.

A TOOL FOR THE VERY YOUNG

As FORTH demonstrated, the advent of the microcomputer served to spread not only the straightforward teaching languages, BASIC and Pascal, but some unconventional ones as well. Perhaps the most dramatic instance of the effect of the microcomputer on the language revolution involves Logo, a language so easy to use that three-year-old children have learned to create programs with it. Logo is best known as the language with the "turtle" built in. The turtle is a triangular character that appears on the computer screen and moves in response to commands typed on the keyboard *(pages 108-109)*. Children — or any other users — learn to create programs that draw simple geometric figures such as a triangle or a

From its base at Kitt Peak, Arizona, the National Radio Astronomy Observatory's 36-foot radio telescope tracks the stars under the control of computers programmed in FORTH, a language developed by astronomer Charles Moore in the early 1970s. Since then, FORTH has been widely adopted by others interested in programming computers to manipulate a variety of scientific instruments and machines.

Learning Concepts from Logo's Turtle

Since its development in the late 1960s, Logo has become widely known as a powerful language for teaching young children concepts in mathematics, geometry and computer programming, largely through the use of so-called turtle graphics. Beginners build their skills one step at a time by manipulating a triangular onscreen character known as the turtle *(below)*. At first, the programmer may give the turtle simple orders such as FORWARD 100, meaning "Move forward 100 steps," or LEFT 60, meaning "Make a 60-degree left turn." The commands may then be used to create small programs, or procedures, for drawing geometric shapes, such as circles and squares, which in turn can be combined to make more complex procedures and shapes.

Like its parent language, LISP, Logo is extensible. In addition to possessing built-in operations such as FORWARD, RIGHT and LEFT, Logo allows the programmer to define new

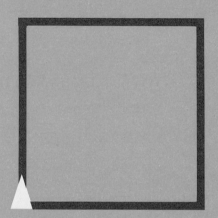

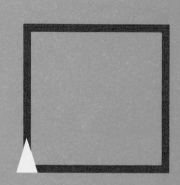

```
TO SQUARE1
FORWARD 100
RIGHT 90
FORWARD 100
RIGHT 90
FORWARD 100
RIGHT 90
FORWARD 100
RIGHT 90
END
```

? SQUARE1

Using Logo's turtle graphics, a novice programmer might draw a square by inventing a procedure named TO SQUARE1 (the 1 here simply indicates that other procedures for drawing squares will be shown). The procedure's commands direct the screen turtle's movements according to the values given in each step. Thus, the turtle goes forward 100 steps, makes a 90-degree right turn and so on until the procedure ends and the square is formed.

```
TO SQUARE2
REPEAT 4 [FORWARD 100 RIGHT 90]
END
```

? SQUARE2

A more advanced Logo programmer learns to avoid redundancy — thus saving space in memory and avoiding potential typing errors — by using the repeat command, as illustrated in the procedure TO SQUARE2. The turtle is instructed to repeat the bracketed instructions four times, to form a square identical to the first one. However, the procedure itself takes only three lines to write instead of 10.

```
TO SQUARE :SIZE
REPEAT 4 [FORWARD :SIZE RIGHT 90]
END
```

? SQUARE 80

The procedure TO SQUARE :SIZE illustrates the use of a variable, represented by placing a colon before a word. This tells the turtle to get the variable's value and plug it in as indicated. Here, :SIZE is the length of a side, allowing the programmer to create a square of any size by assigning a value when the procedure is run. In this case, :SIZE is designated as 80 steps, making a smaller square than those at left.

procedures. The word TO — as in TO SQUARE — signals that a procedure is about to be defined: The next word is the name of the procedure, with END marking the end of the definition; in between are one or more instructions. Once a procedure has been defined, it becomes part of the computer's vocabulary; typing the procedure's name causes the computer to execute the instructions. Not only may a procedure be invoked within another procedure, as shown here; it may also be called upon within itself, recursively *(pages 74-75)*, allowing complicated programs to be written in compact form.

Another aspect of Logo that makes it easy to learn is that the language does not require types of variables to be declared beforehand, as would be necessary in a Pascal program, for instance *(pages 52-53)*. Instead, variables are simply identified by a colon in front of a word. In writing the procedure TO SQUARE :SIZE shown below, third from left, the programmer simply included the variable :SIZE as applying to the procedure, without having to say whether :SIZE is an integer, a real number or a character string. In the turtle-graphics procedures here, typing SQUARE 80 would then produce a square 80 units on a side; in another Logo program, SQUARE 80 might produce the result of multiplying 80 by itself.

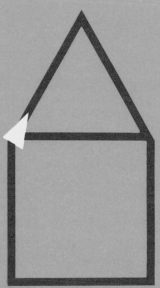

```
TO TRIANGLE :SIZE
REPEAT 3 [FORWARD :SIZE RIGHT 120]
END


? TRIANGLE 80
```

Using variables and the repeat command, the programmer can build other procedures to create other shapes. The procedure shown here yields an equilateral triangle by repeating the command in brackets three times. When the procedure is run, the variable :SIZE, representing the length of each side, is assigned the value of 80 steps.

```
TO HOUSE :SIZE
SQUARE :SIZE
TRIANGLE :SIZE
END


? HOUSE 80
```

When procedures are combined to create more complex shapes, unexpected bugs may occur. The goal of TO HOUSE :SIZE was to draw a square house with a triangle roof. Instead, the triangle ends up inside the square. This happens because at the end of the squaring procedure the turtle has returned to the start *(the lower left corner)* and is pointing straight up; thus when it begins the triangle, it draws one oriented like the triangle at left.

```
TO GOODHOUSE :SIZE
RIGHT 90
SQUARE :SIZE
LEFT 60
TRIANGLE :SIZE
END


? GOODHOUSE 80
```

The procedure TO GOODHOUSE :SIZE corrects the error by turning the turtle 90 degrees to the right before starting the procedure TO SQUARE :SIZE. When the turtle has finished the square — which is now located in the lower part of the screen — it is once again facing right. Before beginning TO TRIANGLE :SIZE, the turtle must be turned 60 degrees to the left to position the triangle on top of the square, where the roof belongs.

square, and combine these programs into bigger programs to build more complex figures, such as a house. Before long, the children have taught themselves simultaneous lessons in art, geometry and computer programming.

Logo was designed in the late 1960s at M.I.T. under the direction of mathematics and education professor Seymour Papert. An ardent student of how the mind works and learns, Papert once wrote that he "always considered learning a hobby." To pursue that hobby, he has taught himself such diverse skills as flying airplanes, reading Chinese and juggling. Papert also thinks about thinking with such intensity that, like the classic absent-minded professor, he sometimes loses touch with the everyday world: Once he flew halfway across the Atlantic before realizing he had left his wife at the airport in New York. A native of South Africa, where as a boy he published a mimeographed newspaper protesting apartheid, Papert earned doctorates in mathematics in his homeland and at Cambridge University. He then spent five years in Geneva working with the noted Swiss psychologist Jean Piaget, whose theory that children learn primarily by manipulating their environment greatly influenced him. In recalling his own boyhood fascination with automobile gears, for example, Papert concluded that the gears had provided him with a concrete "object-to-think-with" and eased his later entry into the abstractions of mathematics.

FROM GEARS TO COMPUTERS

Realizing that computers might similarly provide children with tools for thought, he joined M.I.T.'s Artificial Intelligence Laboratory in 1964 to pursue this line of investigation. Papert was convinced that children of grade-school age and younger could learn to program. "Learning languages is one of the things children do best," he said. "Every normal child learns to talk. Why then should a child not learn to 'talk' to a computer?" But Papert also believed that even BASIC, the simplest computer language then in existence, was too abstract for young children. So he and his colleagues derived a new language from LISP, naming it Logo, from the Greek for "word." It was Papert's inspired addition of the turtle concept as an inviting "object-to-think-with" — first in the form of a mechanical turtle crawling on the floor and then as an onscreen graphic — that gave the language its charm and irresistible appeal to children. In most computer-aided instruction, Papert has pointed out, "the computer is used to put children through their paces." The computer, in effect, programs the child. Logo, by contrast, "convinces the child that he can master the machine. It lets him say, 'I'm the boss.' "

Designed originally for M.I.T.'s expensive mainframes and minicomputers, Logo has since spread into thousands of elementary-school classrooms; now children can blithely learn the program-writing art that only a generation earlier had been the restricted domain of a few highly trained mathematicians. In the process, the youngsters open mental doors and discover, as one of them told Papert, "new rooms in my mind."

Logo designer Seymour Papert of M.I.T. demonstrates the mechanical counterpart of the language's onscreen turtle cursor. Young Logo users learn to write programs by building on simple commands that direct the pen-equipped toy turtle to move forward or backward and turn left or right to sketch images such as this fish.

Two Departures from Language Traditions

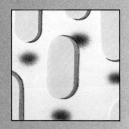

In every high-level language, the language's editing and translating programs combine with the hardware of a computer to accomplish the job that needs to be done. This combination of hardware and software creates a so-called virtual computer, a machine with sophisticated data structures for storing information and powerful procedures for manipulating it. In effect, the virtual computer transforms a language's characteristic approach to problem solving into a particular computing environment. Different kinds of language can create widely varying environments, even when used with the same hardware.

For many years the most common environment was that created by procedural languages, such as FORTRAN, Pascal and Ada. Programs in these languages are built from two distinct elements: data and procedures. The programmer stores data in the computer and then gives the computer a step-by-step list of the procedures to follow in solving the problem at hand. But as high-level languages evolved, other language types came into wider use.

Object-oriented languages and descriptive languages, both of which are explained on the following pages, create environments that are radically different from the environment engendered by a procedural language. The difference lies primarily in the fact that many more of the mechanical details of computing are hidden from the programmer. For example, a program written in Prolog — a descriptive language widely used in the field of artificial intelligence — consists only of declarations that define quantities and relationships between objects. The relation *(product height width area)*, for instance, describes the formula *area = height * width*. But instead of spelling out for the computer how to solve the equation for area — or for height when width and area are known — the programmer simply defines the relationship and lets the computer figure out how to find the answer to a given question.

An Environment That Deals in Objects

An object-oriented language establishes a computing environment populated by many independent objects, each having its own characteristics and ways of interacting with other objects. In this environment, an object behaves, in effect, like a computer; it is capable of receiving messages from other objects, storing information and manipulating the information in limited ways. By structuring the exchange of messages between objects, the programmer can build the complex of operations that makes up a program. And the programmer can employ objects to perform tasks without having to understand the mechanics of each object's performance; an object-oriented language hides much of the detail of a system inside the objects themselves. If necessary, however, the programmer can modify the details contained in an object and can create objects to perform new tasks.

Operations on data are triggered when an object receives a message that names a manipulation to be performed. The specific procedures needed to carry out the named manipulation are contained in the receiving object in a kind of internal program known as a method. A method manipulates data stored in the object and may also send messages to other objects to achieve the desired result, which is then returned to the requesting object.

Every object understands messages related to whatever the object represents. For example, an object that stands for a number can understand messages that request arithmetic computations. An object that represents a list, in contrast, has no need to understand such computations; instead, it understands messages that call for the storing or retrieving of information. An object that stands for a shape on a computer screen knows how to respond to messages that inquire about the shape's location and size.

An object-oriented language is well suited to writing the complicated programs that control computer systems. Because each component of the system can be represented as an object, the replacement of one element, such as the software that controls a printer or monitor, can be accommodated in the programming without changes to any other part of the system: The programmer simply makes sure that the new component responds to the same messages as the one it replaces; how that response is achieved is immaterial.

In an object-oriented environment, objects resemble small, specialized computers, with their own data and procedures. The programmer can treat an object as an independent entity, having its own name and protocol, or set of messages that cause it to perform computations.

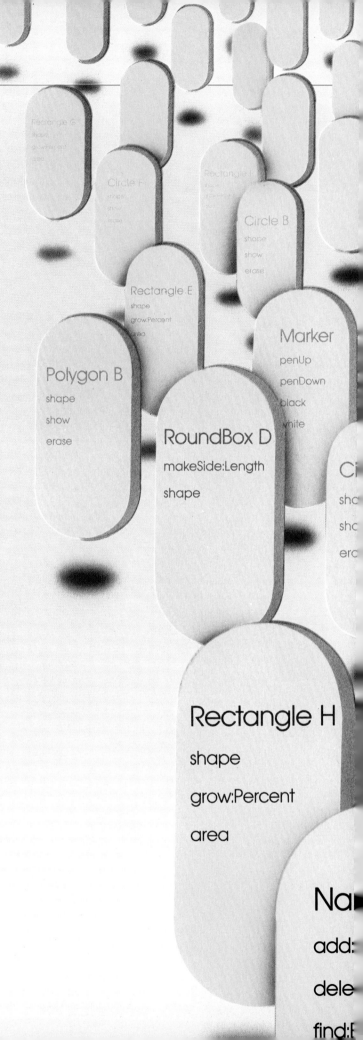

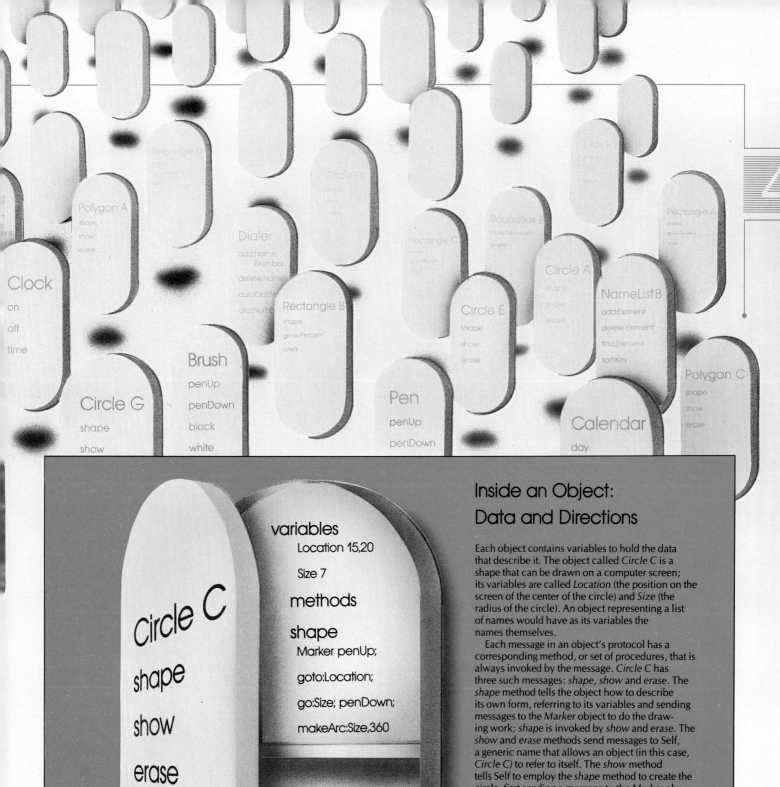

Clock
on
off
time

Polygon A
shapes
show
erase

Dialer
add:Name,
Number
delete:Name
autoDial:
dial:Number

Rectangle B
shape
grow:Percent
area

Brush
penUp
penDown
black
white

Circle G
shape
show

Pen
penUp
penDown

Circle E
shape
show
erase

Circle A
shape
show
erase

NameList B
add:Element
delete:Element
find:Element
sort:Key

Calendar
day

Polygon C
shape
show
erase

Rectangle A
shape
grow:Percent
area

Inside an Object: Data and Directions

Circle C

shape

show

erase

variables
Location 15,20
Size 7

methods
shape
Marker penUp;
goto:Location;
go:Size; penDown;
makeArc:Size,360

show
Marker black
Self shape

erase
Marker white
Self shape

Each object contains variables to hold the data that describe it. The object called *Circle C* is a shape that can be drawn on a computer screen; its variables are called *Location* (the position on the screen of the center of the circle) and *Size* (the radius of the circle). An object representing a list of names would have as its variables the names themselves.

Each message in an object's protocol has a corresponding method, or set of procedures, that is always invoked by the message. *Circle C* has three such messages: *shape, show* and *erase*. The *shape* method tells the object how to describe its own form, referring to its variables and sending messages to the *Marker* object to do the drawing work; *shape* is invoked by *show* and *erase*. The *show* and *erase* methods send messages to Self, a generic name that allows an object (in this case, *Circle C*) to refer to itself. The *show* method tells Self to employ the *shape* method to create the circle, first sending a message to the *Marker* object that tells it to draw black lines. The *erase* method tells Self to use *shape* to delete the circle, with *Marker* drawing white lines.

t A

ent

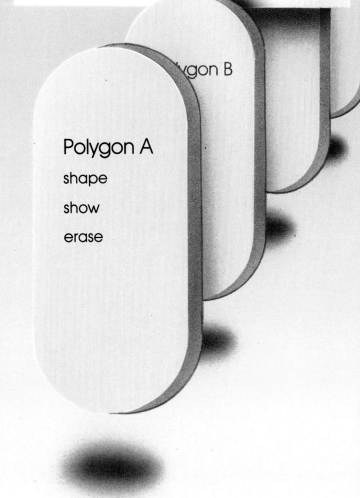

Class	**Object**		
Supercla			
Variables			
Message and methods			

Class	**DisplayObject**		
Superclass	**Object**		
Variables			
Messages and methods			

Class	**Polygon**		
Superclass	**DisplayObject**		
Variables	**Location**	**Sides**	**Length** **Angle**
Messages and methods	**shape**	**show**	**erase**
	Marker penUp Marker goto:Location Marker penDown for n = 1 to Sides [Marker go:Length (n); Markerturn:Angle(n)]	Marker black Self shape	Marker white Self shape

Here, the class named *Object* establishes a property of all objects: that they respond to messages by invoking methods to manipulate their variables.

DisplayObject, a subclass of *Object,* is the blueprint for objects that can be drawn on the screen. It establishes methods for making arcs and lines, and for performing other tasks.

Polygon, a subclass of *DisplayObject,* has variables named *Location, Sides, Length* and *Angle;* some of the messages it responds to are *shape, show* and *erase.*

Polygon B

Polygon A

shape

show

erase

The Simplicity of a Class Structure

Each object in an object-oriented environment possesses independent characteristics, but groups, or classes, of objects share certain properties and behave similarly. The very definition of a class specifies the common properties of its individual members; all have the same number and kind of private variables, respond to the same messages and employ the same methods to manipulate their variables. Members of a class are distinguished from one another by the specific values of their private variables. For example, in response to a given message, each member of a class called *Circle* might be able to change its size as displayed on the screen; but the size would vary according to the value assigned to a member's variable for size.

As illustrated in the simplified object-oriented language at right, classes are organized in a hierarchy of superclasses and subclasses. At the pinnacle is the superclass *Object,* which defines the common properties of all objects, such as their ability to respond to messages. A subclass inherits the messages and methods of the superclasses above it in the hierarchy; a subclass can also incorporate new messages and methods to implement its unique characteristics. A class is also an object in itself; among its methods is one for creating a new member of the class. For example, a programmer (or another object) can send a message to a class called *Rectangle,* telling it to create a new member, *BoxA,* and specifying the size and location of the new member of the class. *BoxA* will incorporate all the methods of class *Rectangle;* but its private variables for size and location will hold unique values.

114

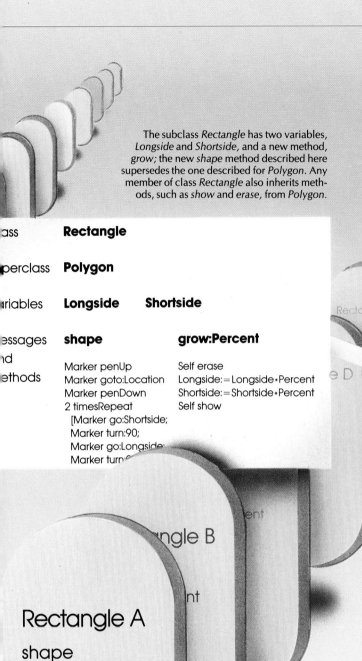

The subclass *Rectangle* has two variables, *Longside* and *Shortside,* and a new method, *grow;* the new *shape* method described here supersedes the one described for *Polygon.* Any member of class *Rectangle* also inherits methods, such as *show* and *erase,* from *Polygon.*

Class	**Rectangle**	
Superclass	**Polygon**	
Variables	**Longside**	**Shortside**
Messages and methods	**shape**	**grow:Percent**
	Marker penUp	Self erase
	Marker goto:Location	Longside:=Longside*Percent
	Marker penDown	Shortside:=Shortside*Percent
	2 timesRepeat	Self show
	[Marker go:Shortside;	
	Marker turn:90;	
	Marker go:Longside;	
	Marker turn:	

The subclass *RoundBox* has a new variable, *ArcSize;* other variables are inherited from *Rectangle.* A new *shape* method uses the brand-new method *makeSide* to draw a side with a rounded corner; the methods *show* and *erase* are inherited from *Polygon.*

Class	**RoundBox**	
Superclass	**Rectangle**	
Variables	**ArcSize**	
Messages and methods	**makeSide:Length**	**shape**
	Marker go:Length−(2*ArcSize)	Marker penUp
	Marker makeArc:ArcSize,90	Marker goto:Location
		Marker go:ArcSize
		Marker penDown
		2 timesRepeat
		[makeSide:Shortside;
		makeSide:Longside]

Rectangle A
shape
grow:Percent

RoundBox A
shape

"What is the area of Rectangle B?"

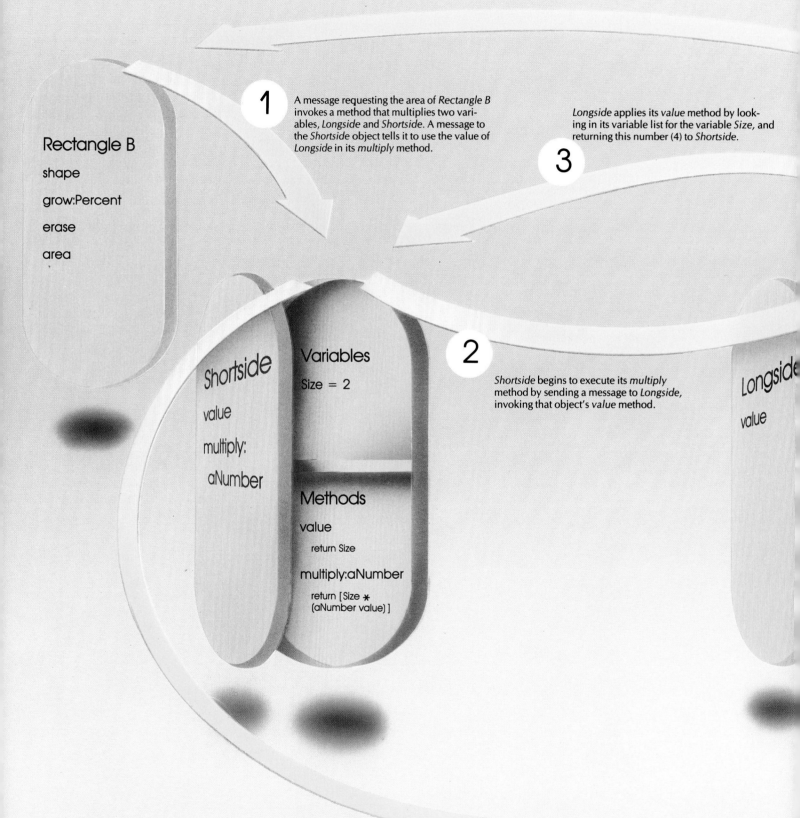

Rectangle B

shape

grow:Percent

erase

area

1 A message requesting the area of *Rectangle B* invokes a method that multiplies two variables, *Longside* and *Shortside*. A message to the *Shortside* object tells it to use the value of *Longside* in its *multiply* method.

3 *Longside* applies its *value* method by looking in its variable list for the variable *Size,* and returning this number (4) to *Shortside*.

Shortside

value

multiply:

　aNumber

Variables

Size = 2

Methods

value

　return Size

multiply:aNumber

　return [Size *
　(aNumber value)]

2 *Shortside* begins to execute its *multiply* method by sending a message to *Longside,* invoking that object's *value* method.

Longside

value

Sending Messages to Call for Action

A program written in an object-oriented language does not contain a universally available list of the attributes of all of its objects; rather, each object keeps track of its own attributes. In addition, no external procedures can act directly on an object's data. The only way to get information about an object or to manipulate its data is by sending messages that invoke the object's methods, which in turn act on the object's variables. Since all members of a class share the same methods, it is the different values of these variables that make the members respond in different ways to given messages.

All but the most basic objects, such as numbers, are microcosms of the object-oriented environment, containing a number of variables that are themselves objects capable of performing manipulations. Thus, the execution of a method — even one that refers only to an object's own variables — usually involves the sending of more messages. In the example shown here, which might occur in an educational program, an object representing a rectangular shape receives a message requesting the value of its area. The method corresponding to that message entails sending a message to one of the rectangle's variables and awaiting its response.

5

The temporary object reports its contents to *Rectangle B,* which can then complete its *area* method by returning the result of the multiplication to whatever external object invoked the method.

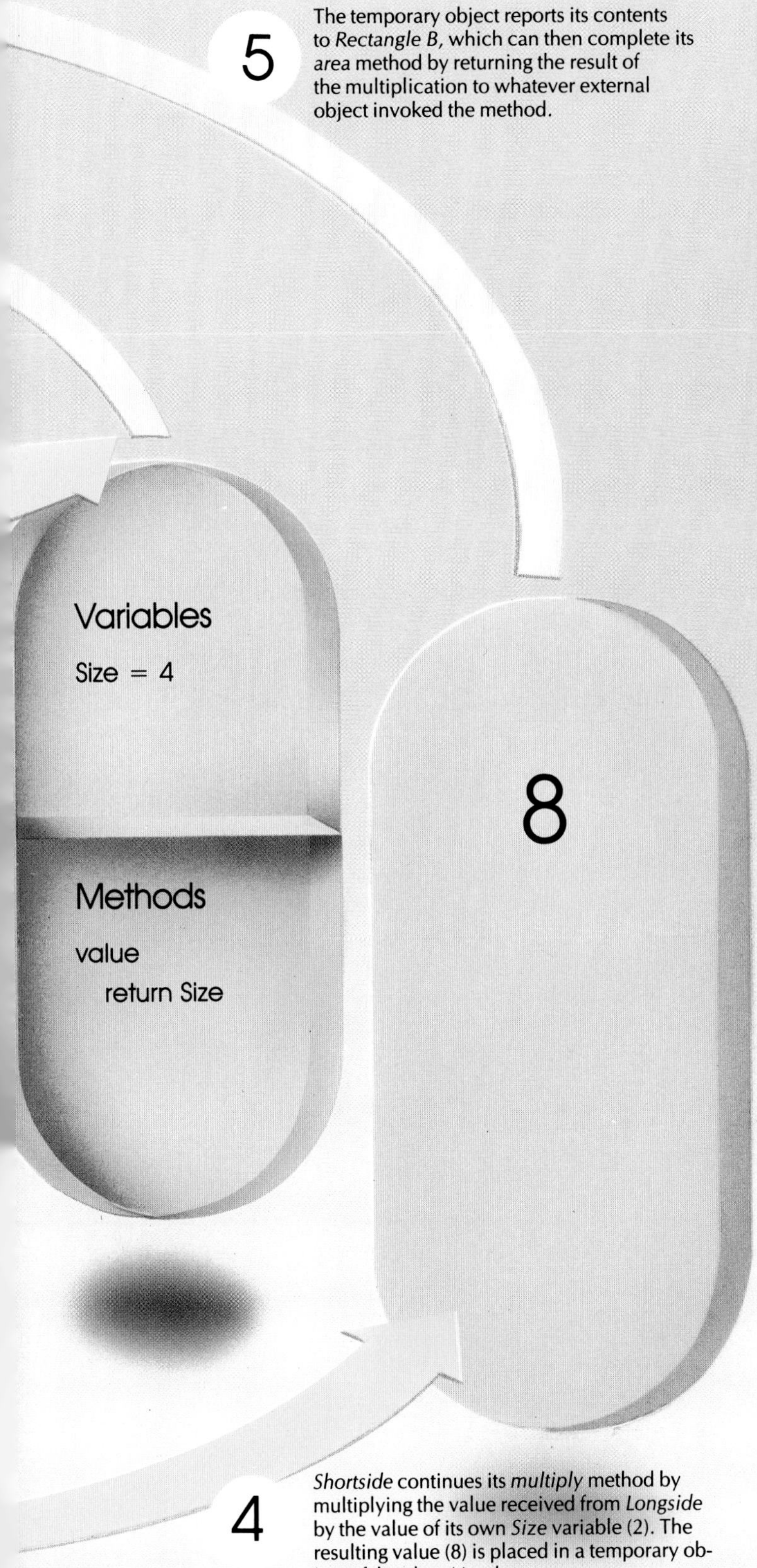

Variables

Size = 4

Methods

value
    return Size

8

4

Shortside continues its *multiply* method by multiplying the value received from *Longside* by the value of its own *Size* variable (2). The resulting value (8) is placed in a temporary object of the class *Number.*

Descriptive Languages: Nothing but the Facts

A descriptive language hides virtually all procedures from the programmer: Instead of having to prescribe a set of procedures that solve a problem step by step, a programmer working in a descriptive language builds a data base of facts relevant to the problem, then poses questions about the facts. The language translator sifts through the facts until it arrives at a solution or determines that not enough in-

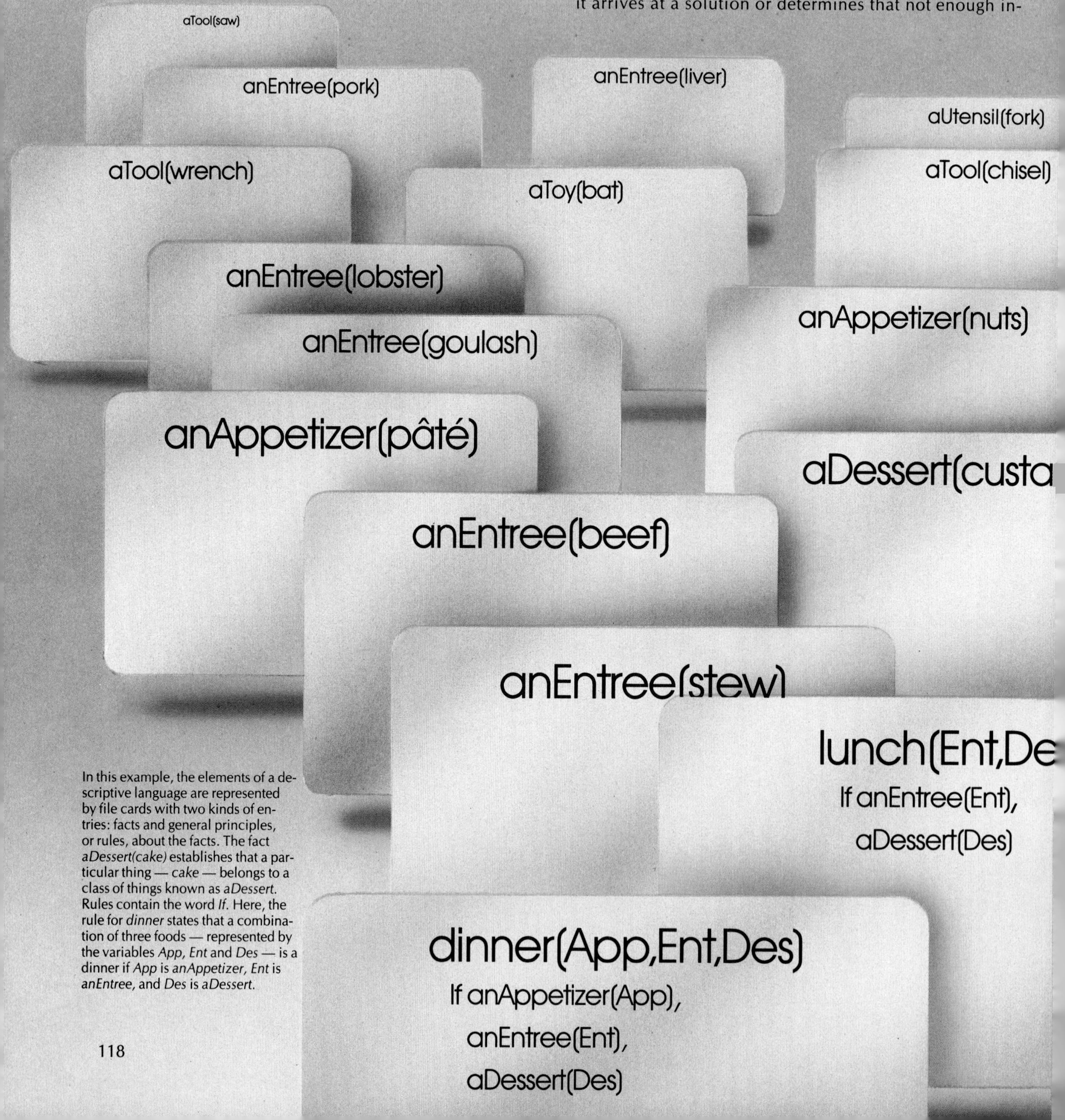

aTool(saw)

anEntree(pork)

anEntree(liver)

aUtensil(fork)

aTool(wrench)

aToy(bat)

aTool(chisel)

anEntree(lobster)

anEntree(goulash)

anAppetizer(nuts)

anAppetizer(pâté)

aDessert(custa

anEntree(beef)

anEntree(stew)

lunch(Ent,De

If anEntree(Ent),

aDessert(Des)

In this example, the elements of a descriptive language are represented by file cards with two kinds of entries: facts and general principles, or rules, about the facts. The fact *aDessert(cake)* establishes that a particular thing — *cake* — belongs to a class of things known as *aDessert*. Rules contain the word *If*. Here, the rule for *dinner* states that a combination of three foods — represented by the variables *App, Ent* and *Des* — is a dinner if *App* is *anAppetizer, Ent* is *anEntree*, and *Des* is *aDessert*.

dinner(App,Ent,Des)

If anAppetizer(App),

anEntree(Ent),

aDessert(Des)

formation has been provided to make a solution possible.

A descriptive-language program has two parts: a data base and a goal. The data base contains particular facts about the problem to be solved and general principles concerning relationships among those facts. The goal is a general description of the solution; in stating the goal, a programmer in effect asks the computer to look at the facts and relationships and to combine them in such a way as to prove that the goal is true.

One growing application of descriptive languages is in the development of expert systems. An expert system is a program that provides advice and limited decision-making on a particular subject by drawing on a large quantity of facts related to the subject.

anEntree(ham)

snack(App,Des)
If anAppetizer(App),
'Des)

aToy(ball)

aTool(hammer)

aUtensil(knife)

aToy(kaleidoscope)

anEntree(chicken)

anAppetizer(cheese)

aUtensil(spoon)

anEntree(veal)

anAppetizer(shrimp)

anEntree(swordfish)

anAppetizer(melon)

aDessert(cake)

"Find a dinner menu with melon as an appetizer."

The translator may do preliminary sorting of the data before the program runs. In effect, it groups all relationships together and also associates similar facts with one another.

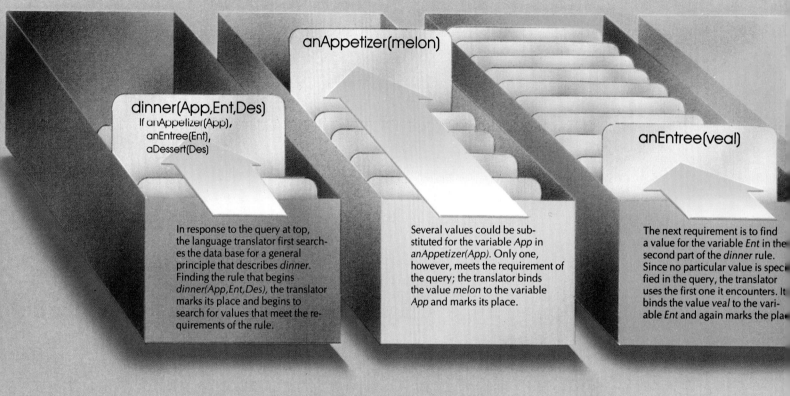

anAppetizer(melon)

dinner(App,Ent,Des)
If anAppetizer(App),
anEntree(Ent),
aDessert(Des)

anEntree(veal)

In response to the query at top, the language translator first searches the data base for a general principle that describes *dinner*. Finding the rule that begins *dinner(App,Ent,Des)*, the translator marks its place and begins to search for values that meet the requirements of the rule.

Several values could be substituted for the variable *App* in *anAppetizer(App)*. Only one, however, meets the requirement of the query; the translator binds the value *melon* to the variable *App* and marks its place.

The next requirement is to find a value for the variable *Ent* in the second part of the *dinner* rule. Since no particular value is specified in the query, the translator uses the first one it encounters. It binds the value *veal* to the variable *Ent* and again marks the pla...

"Find another dinner menu."

Asked for another menu, the translator goes to the place where it answered the previous query and begins searching further. Moving through the dessert collection, it finds *aDessert(custard)*. Once again, all the requirements for a dinner have been met, and the translator reports to the user *App = melon; Ent = veal; Des = custard.*

anAppetizer(melon)

dinner(App,Ent,Des)
If anAppetizer(App),
anEntree(Ent),
aDessert(Des)

anEntree(veal)

aDessert(custard)

A Methodical Search for Solutions

When a program written in a descriptive language is running, the language translator operates by first trying to match the user's query, or goal, with one of the general principles, or rules, in the program's data base. It then goes through the facts in the data base and tries to substitute specific values for the variables in the rule. If the translator finds a rule and a set of facts that match the terms of the query, it reports them to the user; otherwise, it reports the failure of the search.

Generally, the translator follows a prescribed pattern in trying to answer the user's query. In the example shown here, after matching the query to a rule, the translator seeks appropriate values for each element of the rule in sequence, moving from left to right, until it has satisfied all requirements. When the query is repeated, a process called backtracking comes into play. Instead of starting its search all the way back at the beginning, the translator backs up only to the place in the data base where it found the last suitable value. It then finds a replacement value for this element to satisfy the requirements of the rule. If a replacement cannot be found at this point, further backtracking occurs.

aDessert(cake)

Going to the desserts, the translator fulfills the final requirement of the rule by binding the value *cake* to the variable *Des*. The translator can now report back to the user: *App = melon; Ent = veal; Des = cake.*

"And another."

Asked for one more example, the translator again starts where it satisfied the previous query, but all dessert entries have been used. It then backtracks to the marker where it fulfilled the preceding subgoal, for entrees. Finding *anEntree(swordfish)*, the translator returns to the desserts, where it begins again, finding *aDessert(cake)*. Now it can report *App = melon; Ent = swordfish; Des = cake.*

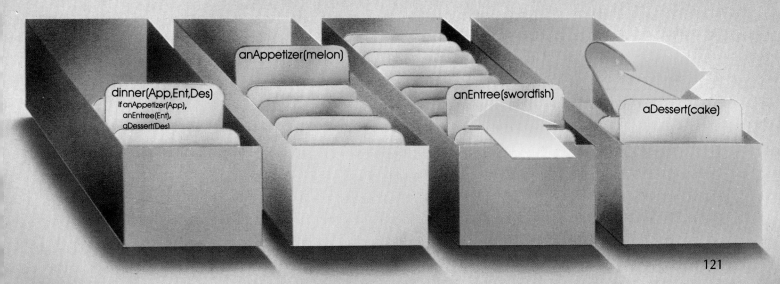

dinner(App,Ent,Des)
If anAppetizer(App),
anEntree(Ent),
aDessert(Des)

anAppetizer(melon)

anEntree(swordfish)

aDessert(cake)

Glossary

Address: the numbered location of a specific cell in a computer's memory.

Algorithm: a step-by-step procedure for solving a problem; programming languages are essentially means of expressing algorithms.

Array: a data structure containing elements that have some feature in common; the computer equivalent of a table of information.

Artificial intelligence (AI): the branch of computer science that attempts to create programs capable of emulating such human characteristics as learning and reasoning.

Assembler: a program that converts the mnemonic instructions of assembly-language programs into the zeros and ones of binary machine code.

Assembly language: a low-level programming language, specific to a given computer, that uses short mnemonics corresponding directly to machine instructions and that allows a programmer to use symbolic addresses.

Binary code: a system for representing information by combinations of two symbols, such as one and zero, true and false, or the presence or absence of voltage.

Binary number system: a number system that uses two as its base and expresses numbers as sequences of zeros and ones.

Bit: the smallest unit of information in a digital computer, equivalent to a single zero or one. The word "bit" is a contraction of "binary digit."

Block structure: the division of a program into self-contained units; used for writing and testing parts of programs separately.

Boolean: a data type, sometimes called a logical, that allows one of two values: true or false. Named for 19th-century English mathematician George Boole.

Central processing unit (CPU): the part of the computer that executes instructions.

Clock: a device, usually based on a quartz crystal, that gives off regular pulses used to coordinate a computer's operations.

Compiler: a program that converts a program written in a high-level language into either machine code or assembly language, holding the instructions in memory without executing them; the compiled program is stored for use at any later time. *See also* interpreter.

Computer language: *see* programming language.

Constant: a declared value that remains unchanged during the execution of a program.

Data structure: a collection of data in which related elements are referred to by a common name in order to organize, store and retrieve the information efficiently.

Data type: the classification of a constant, variable or element according to whether it will hold an integer, string, real number or Boolean.

Declaration: a series of statements that identifies the data structures and types of data that a program will manipulate.

Dialect: a variation of a programming language that tailors the language to a certain application or to exploit the strengths of a particular computer.

Digital: pertaining to the representation, manipulation or transmission of information by discrete signals.

Extension: an expanded version of a language supplemented with features that increase the language's capabilities.

Function: a type of subroutine that produces a single value and is frequently employed for mathematical operations such as square or square root; in most languages, more commonly used operations such as addition or subtraction are represented by operators.

Hexadecimal (Hex): a number system, based on 16, in which a single digit represents four binary digits.

High-level language: a programming language that approximates human language more closely than does machine code or assembly language, and in which one statement may invoke several machine-code or assembly-language instructions.

Identifier: a label given to a constant, variable or data structure that identifies it to the computer.

Input: information fed into a computer.

Instruction: an elementary machine-code or assembly-language order to a computer's central processing unit specifying an operation to be carried out by the computer; a sequence of instructions forms a program.

Instruction cycle: the series of activities a computer performs in order to read an instruction from memory, decode it, execute it and prepare for the next instruction.

Integer: in computer science, a data type consisting of zero and both positive and negative whole numbers; also known as a whole number.

Interpreter: a program that translates a program written in a high-level language every time the high-level program is to be executed. *See also* compiler.

Keyword: a word in a programming language that has a specific meaning to the compiler or interpreter and thus cannot be used for any other purpose in a program written in that langugage.

List-processing language: a type of programming language that represents data in lists of words and other symbols in order to link concepts in a manner roughly analogous to the way they may be linked in the human brain; programs in a list-processing language may consist simply of lists.

Loop: a technique that allows a program to repeat a series of instructions a number of times.

Machine code: a set of binary digits that can be directly understood by a computer without translation.

Machine-independent: a characteristic of a language that allows its programs to be translated and run on computers of different design.

Memory: the principal work space inside a computer in which data can be recorded or from which it is retrieved; the term applies to internal storage facilities as opposed to external storage, such as disks or tapes.

Mnemonic: a short term or symbol used to designate an instruction or operation.

Nonprocedural language: a language that allows a programmer to describe the desired result of a program without having to specify how to obtain it.

Object code: the machine-code output of a compiler.

Object-oriented language: a type of programming language that represents information in units called objects, each containing data and a set of operations to manipulate that data.

Octal: a number system, based on eight, in which a single digit represents three binary digits.

Opcode: the part of an assembly-language instruction that tells a computer what operation is to be performed; the word "opcode" is a contraction of "operating code."

Operand: the part of an assembly-language instruction that gives the computer the address of the data to be operated on.

Operating system: a set of programs used to control, assist or supervise all other programs that run on a computer system.

Operation: an action performed by a computer in response to an instruction.

Operator: a word or symbol in a high-level language that represents mathematical operations, logical comparisons or other operations on data; for example, + is commonly used as the operator for addition.

Optimizer: the part of a compiler that attempts to shorten or reorganize object code so that it occupies less space in memory or runs faster when it is executed.

Output: the result of a computation, presented by a computer to the user, to another computer or to some form of storage.

Procedural language: a programming language that requires sequences of explicit instructions for arriving at a desired solution.

Procedure: *see* subroutine.

Program: a sequence of instructions for performing some operation or solving some problem by computer.

Programming language: a set of words, letters, numerals and abbreviated mnemonics, regulated by a specific syntax, used to describe a program to a computer.

Real number: in computer science, a data type consisting of numbers written with a decimal point and/or an exponent.

Record: a data structure containing different but logically related items that are treated as a unit.

Recursion: the ability of a program to refer to itself as a subroutine.

Reserved word: *see* keyword.

Software: programs that enable a computer to do useful work.

Source code: the lines of programming in a high-level language that are fed to a compiler or interpreter to be translated into machine code or assembly language.

Statement: an instruction in a high-level program that tells the computer what to do.

String: a series of characters, often a name or word.

Structured programming: a systematic approach to the creation of software; in particular, it calls for dividing programs into small, independent tasks.

Subroutine: a self-contained section of a computer program that can be separately prepared and referred to by a single name. When the name of a subroutine appears as a statement in a program, the entire group of statements that it represents is executed.

Subset: a limited version of a language that contains only some of the features of the full language.

Symbolic address: a word in an assembly-language program that is used instead of a number to refer to an address in memory.

Syntax: the rules for arranging words and symbols in a programming language in a manner that is understandable to the language's compiler or interpreter.

Variable: a declared element whose value may be changed during a program's execution. *See also* constant.

Bibliography

Books

Aguado-Muñoz, Ricardo, et al., *BASIC Básico Curso de Programación*. Madrid: Grupo Distribuidor Editorial, 1982.

Al-Daffa, Ali Abdullah, *The Muslim Contribution to Mathematics*. London: Croom Helm, 1977.

Bates, William, *The Computer Cookbook*. Garden City, N.Y.: Doubleday, Quantum Press, 1984.

Bitter, Gary G., *Computers in Today's World*. New York: John Wiley & Sons, 1984.

Booch, Grady, *Software Engineering with Ada*. Menlo Park, Calif.: Benjamin/Cummings Publishing, 1983.

Bosak, Jon, *Executive Briefing: Ada*. Reston, Va.: Longman Crown Group, 1984.

British Computer Society, The, *High Level Programming Languages: The Way Ahead*. Manchester, England: NCC Publications, 1973.

Cashman, Thomas J., and Gary B. Shelly, *Introduction to Computers and Data Processing*. Fullerton, Calif.: Anaheim Publishing, 1980.

Chirlian, Paul M., *Understanding Computers*. Beaverton, Ore.: Dilithium Press, 1978.

Dijkstra, Edsger W., *Selected Writings on Computing: A Personal Perspective*. New York: Springer-Verlag, 1982.

Dirksen, A. J., *Microcomputers: What They Are and How to Put Them to Productive Use*. Blue Ridge Summit, Pa.: TAB Books, 1978.

Ditlea, Steve, ed., *Digital Deli*. New York: Workman Publishing, 1984.

Dodd, Kenneth Nielson, *Computer Programming and Languages*. London: Butterworths, 1969.

Eisenbach, Susan, and Christopher Sadler, *PASCAL for Programmers*. New York: Springer-Verlag, 1981.

Elson, Mark, *Concepts of Programming Languages*. Science Research Associates, 1973.

Falkoff, Adin D., and Kenneth E. Iverson, *A Source Book in APL*. Palo Alto, Calif.: APL Press, 1981.

Frude, Neil, *The Intimate Machine: Close Encounters with Computers and Robots*. New York: New American Library, 1983.

Gallo, Michael A., and Robert B. Nenno, *Computers and Society with BASIC and Pascal*. Boston: Prindle, Weber and Schmidt, 1985.

Glaser, Anton, *History of Binary and Other Nondecimal Numeration*. Los Angeles: Tomash Publishers, 1981.

Halpern, Mark I., and Christopher J. Shaw, eds., *Annual Review in Automatic Programming 5*. New York: Pergamon Press, 1969.

Heath, Sir Thomas L., *The Thirteen Books of Euclid's Elements*. Vol. 2, Books 3-9. New York: Dover Publications, 1956.

Helms, Harry, ed., *IBM: The McGraw-Hill Computer Handbook*. New York: McGraw-Hill, 1983.

High Level Languages: International Computer State of the Art Report. Maidenhead, Berkshire, England: Infotech Information, 1972.

Hofeditz, Calvin A., *Computer Programming Languages Made Simple*. Garden City, N.Y.: Doubleday, 1984.

Horowitz, Ellis, *Fundamentals of Programming Languages*. Rockville, Md.: Computer Science Press, 1984.

Horowitz, Ellis, ed., *Programming Languages: A Grand Tour*. Rockville, Md.: Computer Science Press, 1983.

Jacker, Corinne, *Man, Memory and Machines: An Introduction to Cybernetics*. New York: Macmillan, 1964.

Katzan, Harry, Jr., *Introduction to Computer Science*. New York: Petrocelli/Charter, 1975.

Kemeny, John G., *Man and the Computer*. New York: Charles Scribner's Sons, 1972.

Knuth, Donald E., *The Art of Computer Programming*. Vol. 2. Reading, Mass.: Addison-Wesley, 1971.

Lampton, Christopher, *Computer Languages*. New York: Franklin Watts, 1983.

Levy, Steven, *Hackers: Heroes of the Computer Revolution*. Garden City, N.Y.: Doubleday, Anchor Press, 1984.

Lord, Walter, *A Night to Remember*. New York: Holt, Rinehart and Winston, 1955.

McCorduck, Pamela, *Machines Who Think*. San Francisco, Calif.: W. H. Freeman, 1979.

Metropolis, N., J. Howlett and Gian-Carlo Rota, eds., *A History of Computing in the Twentieth Century*. New York: Academic Press, 1980.

Miller, George A., *The Psychology of Communication: Seven Essays*. Baltimore: Penguin Books, 1969.

Moll, Robert, and Rachel Folsom, *Apple II Instant Pascal: An Introduction to Programming*. Boston: Houghton Mifflin, 1985.

Neugebauer, Otto, *The Exact Sciences in Antiquity*. Providence, R.I.: Brown University Press, 1957.

Osborne, Adam, and David Bunnell, *An Introduction to Microcomputers*. Vol. 0, *The Beginner's Book*. Berkeley, Calif.: McGraw-Hill, 1982.

Papert, Seymour, *Mindstorms: Children, Computers and Powerful Ideas*. New York: Basic Books, 1980.

Ralston, Anthony, and Edwin D. Reilly Jr., eds., *Encyclopedia of Computer Science and Engineering*. New York: Van Nostrand Reinhold, 1983.

Richards, Martin, and Colin Whitby-Stevens, *BCPL: The Language and Its Compiler*. New York: Cambridge University Press, 1979.

Rosen, Frederic, ed., *The Algebra of Mohammed Ben Musa*. London: The Oriental Translation Fund, 1831.

Sammet, Jean E., *Programming Languages: History and Fundamentals*. Englewood Cliffs, N.J.: Prentice-Hall, 1969.

Seidman, Arthur H., and Ivan Flores, eds., *The Handbook of Computers and Computing*. New York: Van Nostrand Reinhold, 1984.

Stiegler, Marc, and Bob Hansen, *Programming Languages: Featuring the IBM PC and Compatibles*. New York: Baen Enterprises, 1984.

Taylor, Charles F., *The Master Handbook of High-Level Microcomputer Languages*. Blue Ridge Summit, Pa.: TAB Books, 1984.

Time-Life Books Inc., *The Time-Life Step-by-Step Guide to the IBM PC*. New York: Random House, 1984.

Traister, Robert J., *Programming in C*. Englewood Cliffs, N.J.: Prentice-Hall, 1984.

Tucker, Allen B., *Programming Languages*. New York: McGraw-Hill, 1986.

Wasserman, Anthony I., *Tutorial: Programming Language Design*. New York: Computer Society Press, 1980.

Wexelblat, Richard L., ed., *History of Programming Languages*. New York: Academic Press, 1981.

Zaks, Rodnay, *Introduction to Pascal (Including UCSD PASCAL)*. 2nd ed. rev. Berkeley, Calif.: Sybex, 1981.

Periodicals and Other Publications

Aarons, Richard, "Cover Story: Basic." *PC Magazine*, October 29, 1985.

Abelson, Harold, "A Beginner's Guide to Logo." *BYTE*, August 1982.

Aguilar, Hugh, "BASIC Recursive Techniques." *COMPUTER LANGUAGE*, May 1985.

Albrecht, Robert L., "A Modern-Day Medicine Show." *Datamation*, July 1963.

"Alien Landing." *Time*, November 18, 1985.

Amsterdam, Jonathan:
"An Assembler for VM2." *BYTE*, November 1985.

"Computer Languages of the Future." *Popular Computing*, September 1983.

Angier, Natalie, "After 73 Years, a *Titanic* Find." *Time*, September 16, 1985.

Annals of the History of Computing, October 1985.

Backus, John, "The History of FORTRAN I, II, and III." *Annals of the History of Computing*, July 1979.

Ballard, Robert D., "How We Found *Titanic*." *National Geographic*, December 1985.

Bemer, R. W., "A View of the History of COBOL." *Honeywell Computer Journal*, no date.

Bright, Herb, "FORTRAN Comes to Westinghouse-Bettis, 1957." *Annals of the History of Computing*, July 1979.

Brodie, Leo, "An Interview with Charles Moore — Founder of Forth." *COMPUTER LANGUAGE*, premier issue, 1984.

Campbell-Kelly, Martin:
"The Development of Computer Programming in Britain (1945-1955)." *Annals of the History of Computing*, April 1982.
"Programming the EDSAC: Early Programming Activity at the University of Cambridge." *Annals of the History of Computing*, January 1980.
"Programming the Mark I: Early Programming Activity at the University of Manchester." *Annals of the History of Computing*, April 1980.

Colmerauer, Alain, "Prolog in 10 Figures." *Communications of the ACM*, December 1985.

Conner, Richard L., "COBOL, Your Age is Showing." *Computerworld*, May 14, 1984.

Duntemann, Jeff, "Cover Story: Pascal." *PC Magazine*, October 29, 1985.

Embrey, Glenn, "COBOL." *Popular Computing*, September 1983.

Faflick, Phillip, "Teaching the Turtle New Tricks." *Time*, October 11, 1982.

Harvey, Brian, "Why Logo?" *BYTE*, August 1982.

Hemmes, David, "FORTRANSIT Recollections." *Annals of the History of Computing*, January 1986.

Hoare, C.A.R., "The Emperor's Old Clothes." *Communications of the ACM*, February 1981.

Joyce, James, "A C Language Primer." *BYTE*, August 1983.

Kanner, Mel, "FORTRAN." *Popular Computing*, September 1983.

Kelly, Mahlon G., "BASIC: The Universal Micro Language That's Easy to Learn and Easy to Hate." *Popular Computing*, September 1983.

Kemeny, John G., Thomas E. Kurtz and Brig Elliott, "BASIC Becomes a Structured Language." *COMPUTER LANGUAGE*, premier issue, 1984.

Knuth, Donald E., "Ancient Babylonian Algorithms." *Communications of the ACM*, July 1972.

LaGrow, Craig, "P. J. Plauger Reflects on the History of C." *COMPUTER LANGUAGE*, February 1985.

McCauley, Jim, "Languages for Thinking about Thinking." *Whole Earth Software Review*, Fall 1984.

McCormack, Joel, and Richard Gleaves, "Modula-2: A Worthy Successor to Pascal." *BYTE*, April 1983.

McGrath, Ellie, "Haunting Images of Disaster." *Time*, September 23, 1985.

Machrone, Bill, "Micro-Linguistics: Languages for the PC." *PC Magazine*, September 6, 1983.

Millison, Doug, "BASIC's Kemeny and Kurtz Discuss the Language Today." *COMPUTER LANGUAGE*, October 1985.

Moore, Charles H., "The Evolution of FORTH, an Unusual Language." *BYTE,* August 1980.

Oceanus, Winter 1985/1986.

"Pathfinder." *Think,* July/August 1979.

Paul, Robert J., "An Introduction to Modula-2." *BYTE,* August 1984.

Pearlman, Dara, "FORTH Inspires a Fanatic Following." *Popular Computing,* September 1983.

Petzold, Charles, "Assembler." *PC Magazine,* October 29, 1985.

Pountain, Dick, "POP and SNAP." *BYTE,* October 1984.

Rather, Elizabeth D., "Forth, Programming Language." *Forth Inc.,* January 17, 1986.

Ridley, Regina Starr, "Philippe Kahn: The Man behind the Borland Myth." *COMPUTER LANGUAGE,* August 1985.

Roberts, Bruce, "C." *Popular Computing,* September 1983.

Sammet, Jean E., *An Overview of High-Level Languages.* Bethesda, Md.: IBM Federal Systems Division.

Scientific American, September 1984.

Shammas, Namir Clement, "Jean Ichbiah, Ada's Architect." *COMPUTER LANGUAGE,* November 1985.

Snyder, John, "Recursive Procedures." *COMPUTER LANGUAGE,* April 1985.

Solomon, Cynthia, "Introducing Logo to Children." *BYTE,* August 1982.

Somerson, Paul, "In Defense of BASIC." *PC Magazine,* September 1983.

Spalding, Marti, and Ben Dawson, "Finding the *Titanic.*" *BYTE,* March 1986.

Takara, Ken, "Programming Philosophy: Interviews with Donald Knuth and Niklaus Wirth." *COMPUTER LANGUAGE,* May 1985.

Tesler, Lawrence G., "Programming Languages." *Scientific American,* September 1984.

Tuttle, Joey K., "APL pi: Designing an APL Type Font." *APL Quote Quad,* September 1981.

Tymony, Cy, "A Beginner's Guide to Assembly Language." *Popular Computing,* April 1985.

Wadlow, Tom, "Turbo Pascal." *BYTE,* July 1984.

Wagner, Robert, "COBOL: Pride and Prejudice." *COMPUTER LANGUAGE,* premier issue, 1984.

Walker, Virginia C., "The 25th Anniversary of FORTRAN." *Annals of the History of Computing,* October 1982.

Weinman, William E., "Program in Style." *COMPUTER LANGUAGE,* January 1985.

Wirth, Niklaus:
"Data Structures and Algorithms." *Scientific American,* September 1984.
"History and Goals of Modula-2." *BYTE,* August 1984.

Wolf, Chris, "Serious FORTRAN for the PC." *PC Magazine,* December 24, 1985.

Woteki, Tom, and Alan Freiden, "Pascal." *Popular Computing,* September 1983.

Acknowledgments

The index for this book was prepared by Mel Ingber. The editors also wish to thank: **In France:** Choisy-Le-Roi — Claude Roblez, Société Microdur; Gif sur Yvette — Jacques Hebenstreit and Yves Noyelle, École Supérieure d'Électricité. **In the Netherlands:** Nijmegen — Hanno Wupper, Katholieke Universiteit Nijmegen. **In Switzerland:** Zurich — Niklaus Wirth, Eidgenössische Technische Hochschule. **In the United States:** California — Los Angeles: Ellis Horowitz, University of Southern California; Manhattan Beach: Elizabeth D. Rather, FORTH, Inc.; Menlo Park: Bob Albrecht, Dragon Quest; Mountain View: Steven Muchnick, Sun Microsystems; San Jose: Judy Bauer Gan, IBM Research Laboratory; Stanford: John McCarthy, Stanford University; Connecticut — New Haven: Alan Perlis, Yale University; Trumbull: Richard Wexelblat; District of Columbia — George Atiyeh, Library of Congress; Ruth Baacke, Middle East Institute; Rear Admiral Grace Murray Hopper, Naval Data Automation Command; Uta Merzbach, Smithsonian Institution; Maryland — Bethesda: Jean E. Sammet, IBM; College Park: Dana Nau, University of Maryland; Massachusetts — Waltham: Douglas Ross, SofTech, Inc.; Woods Hole: Nancy Green, Stewart Harris and Kenneth R. Peal, Woods Hole Oceanographic Institution; Virginia — Arlington: John Myrna, V. M. Systems Group; Blacksburg: J.A.N. Lee, Virginia Polytechnic Institute. **In West Germany:** Bochum — Christof Born, University of Bochum; Hunfeld — Konrad Zuse; Munich — Rainer Korbmann, *Chip;* St. Augustin — Siegfried Münch, Gesellschaft für Mathematik und Datenverarbeitung; Stuttgart — Uli Deker, *Bild der Wissenschaft.*

Picture Credits

The sources for the illustrations that appear in this book are listed below. Credits from left to right are separated by semicolons, from top to bottom by dashes.

Cover, 6: Art by Peter Sawyer. 8: Art by William J. Hennessy Jr. 10: Erwin Bohm, courtesy Professor Dr. Konrad Zuse, Hunfeld, West Germany. 17: Tablet, Cliché des Musées Nationaux, Paris. 18: Manuscript, Biblioteca Apostolica Vaticana, Rome. 19: Manuscript, Ms. Huntington 214 (folio 2 Verso, folios 3 Verso & 4 recto), Bodleian Library, Oxford. 20, 21: Smithsonian Institution, Neg. No. 86-2845. 23-35: Art by Wayne Vincent. 36-39: Art by Peter Sawyer. 40: Bob Veltri, courtesy Special Collections Library, Virginia Polytechnic Institute, Blacksburg, Virginia. 43: Courtesy David Hemmes. 44: Mark Sexton, courtesy The Computer Museum, Boston, Massachusetts. 46, 47: Flags, Flag Research Center, Winchester, Massachusetts. 49: John McCarthy. 51-65: Art by Steve Wagoner. 66: Art by Peter Sawyer. 68: From *Programming Languages: History and Fundamentals,* by Jean E. Sammet, © 1969, reprinted by permission of Prentice-Hall, Inc., Englewood Cliffs, New Jersey. 70: Program from *Automatically Programmed Tools,* by S. Hori, IIT Research Institute, Brochure No. AZ-240, November 1963. 72-75: Art by William J. Hennessy Jr. 76: Courtesy Professor Dr. Niklaus Wirth, Zurich. 80-97: Art by Matt McMullen. 98-101: Art by Peter Sawyer. 105: © Ed Kashi 1985. 107: Courtesy NRAO/AUI. 110: Susan Pogany, courtesy The M.I.T. Museum. 111-121: Art by Wayne Vincent.

Index

Time-Life Books Inc.
is a wholly owned subsidiary of
THE TIME INC. BOOK COMPANY

President and Chief Executive Officer: Kelso F. Sutton
President, Time Inc. Books Direct:
Christopher T. Linen

TIME-LIFE BOOKS INC.

EDITOR: George Constable
Executive Editor: Ellen Phillips
Director of Design: Louis Klein
Director of Editorial Resources: Phyllis K. Wise
Director of Photography and Research:
John Conrad Weiser

PRESIDENT: John M. Fahey, Jr.
Senior Vice Presidents: Robert M. DeSena,
Paul R. Stewart, Curtis G. Viebranz, Joseph J. Ward
Vice Presidents: Stephen L. Bair, Bonita L.
Boezeman, Mary P. Donohoe, Stephen L. Goldstein,
Juanita T. James, Andrew P. Kaplan, Trevor Lunn,
Susan J. Maruyama, Robert H. Smith
New Product Development: Yuri Okuda,
Donia Ann Steele
Supervisor of Quality Control: James King

PUBLISHER: Joseph J. Ward

Editorial Operations
Copy Chief: Diane Ullius
Production: Celia Beattie
Library: Louise D. Forstall

Computer Composition: Gordon E. Buck (Manager),
Deborah G. Tait, Monika D. Thayer,
Janet Barnes Syring, Lillian Daniels

Correspondents: Elisabeth Kraemer-Singh (Bonn);
Christina Lieberman (New York); Maria Vincenza
Aloisi (Paris); Ann Natanson (Rome). Valuable
assistance was also provided by Patricia Strathern
(Paris).

UNDERSTANDING COMPUTERS

SERIES DIRECTOR: Roberta Conlan
Series Administrator: Loretta Britten

Editorial Staff for *Computer Languages*
Designer: Ellen Robling
Associate Editors: Jeremy N. P. Ross (pictures);
Thomas H. Flaherty, Peter Pocock (text)
Researchers:
Patti H. Cass
Esther Ferington   *Writers:*
Roxie France-Nuriddin   Ray Jones
Gregory A. McGruder   Lydia Preston
Assistant Designer: Antonio Alcalá
Editorial Assistant: Miriam Newton Morrison
Copy Coordinators: Anthony K. Pordes,
Robert M. S. Somerville
Picture Coordinator: Renée DeSandies

Special Contributors: Ronald H. Bailey, Charles Russ
Miller, Steve Olson, Charles C. Smith (text); Susan
Blair, Tina S. McDowell (research)

THE CONSULTANTS

JOHN BACKUS is a respected pioneer in computer languages and in 1963 was named an IBM Fellow, the company's highest honor for technical achievement.

JOHN L. CUADRADO is president of the consulting firm Octy, Inc., in Virginia and also serves as adjunct associate professor at the Thayer School of Engineering of Dartmouth College.

BRIAN HAYES has written on aspects of computing and programming languages for such periodicals as *Scientific American, COMPUTER LANGUAGE, BYTE* and *Lotus,* and for *The New York Times.*

THOR JOHNSON is with Telesis Strategy Consultants in Rhode Island. His special area of interest is computer graphics and systems software.

NEIL MCELROY, former head of the computer center at the White Oak Laboratory of the Naval Surface Weapons Center, directs the Communications, Control and Audio Group at Avelex in Maryland.

ISABEL NIRENBERG has dealt with a wide range of computer applications, from the analysis of data collected by the Pioneer space probes to the matching of children and families for adoption agencies. She works at the Computer Center at the State University of New York at Albany.

NANCY STERN, a professor of computer information systems at Hofstra University in Hempstead, New York, has published several computer textbooks and numerous articles and monographs on the history of computing.

MARY S. VAN DEUSEN works with LISP/VM at IBM's Thomas J. Watson Research Center in Yorktown Heights, New York. She has served as chair of ACM SIGPLAN and as general chair of language and compiler conferences.

JIM WARREN is the founding editor of the periodical *Dr. Dobb's Journal of Computer Calisthenics & Orthodontia* and the creator of the West Coast Computer Faires. He has been a consultant specializing in small computers since 1968.

MARK WEISER is an associate professor in the Department of Computer Science at the University of Maryland, where he also serves as Associate Chairman for Facilities. Noted for his design of software windows, he is interested in environments for heterogeneous systems.

Library of Congress Cataloging in Publication Data

Computer languages / by the editors of Time-Life Books.
  p. cm.—(Understanding computers)
  Includes bibliographical references.
  1. Programming languages (Electronic computers).
  I. Time-Life Books.   II. Series.
QA76.7.C648 1990   005.13′3—dc20   89-20429 CIP
ISBN 0-8094-7574-X
ISBN 0-8094-7575-8 (lib. bdg.)

For information on and a full description of any Time-Life Books
series listed, please call 1-800-621-7026 or write:
Reader Information
Time-Life Customer Service
P.O. Box C-32068
Richmond, Virginia 23261-2068

REVISIONS STAFF

EDITOR: Lee Hassig

Writer: Esther Ferington
Assistant Designer: Tina Taylor
Copy Coordinator: Anne Farr
Picture Coordinator: Leanne G. Miller

Consultant: Michael R. Williams, a professor of
computer science at the University of Calgary in
Canada, is the author of *A History of Computing
Technology.*